Are You Le
Cash on the Table?

As an investor you have stocks in your portfolio. Those stocks, individually, will go up, down or remain about the same. Nothing really you can do about that. Market forces and corporate actions beyond your control will cause fluctuations in the value of your holdings.

But . . .

There is one important action you can take that will put cash in your brokerage account, today and month after month as time rolls by.

Selling Covered Calls and Naked Puts is a stock market strategy favored by many savvy investors. Here's how it works. Take one of your stocks, Stock ABC, which has a market price of $29. If you will agree to sell that stock (a Call option) for $30 on the third Friday of next month the market will pay you X amount of dollars today (the option premium). That's the money that you are currently leaving on the table. The premium X varies by stock and typically is two to three percent of the stock price.

Think about what can happen when you sell the option. Only one of two things will happen. If the stock price of ABC is above $30 on the third Friday you sell it for $30. That will happen about 30% of the time. The other possibility is that ABC is selling for $30 or less on the third Friday. In that case the option expires and you can sell another Call.

Either way the option premium—Real Cash Money—is in your brokerage account ready to be spent or reinvested.

Continue the process month after month for a constant cash income from your portfolio.

The Naked Put strategy also gives you immediate cash. Using the same example with Stock ABC, which is in your portfolio and has a market price of $29, if you agree to buy additional shares at a discounted price of $27.50 on the third Friday of next month (a Put option) the market will pay you Y amount of dollars today (the option premium). If the stock price is above $27.50 on the third Friday the option expires and you can sell another Put, generating more cash income. If the price does dip below $27.50 then you buy the additional shares and can now sell more Covered Calls. The put premium Y varies by stock and typically is one to three percent of the stock price.

This book will give you the basic skills to master the art of selling Covered Calls and Naked Puts.

Now immediately everyone starts to say: Yes! Right! Show me the money!

To satisfy your curiosity a very useful software program called the VISIONS Portfolio Income Explorer [PIE[1]] is available that will immediately analyze your portfolio for the amount of cash income it can generate right now.

How Much Cash Are You Leaving on the Table Right Now?

On the following page is an example of PIE using the DOW 30 stocks. It shows that with an equal weighting investment of about $12,000 in each DOW stock you could generate a monthly income of over $8,800 per month. The annual return on your investment is over 28 percent. This is without any stock appreciation.

You are receiving Call option premium income for holding the stocks. If they do go up in value then your return is even greater. So if you are holding stocks and hoping that they go up, why not get paid while you wait. These results may amaze you, but once you have read this book and implemented some of the concepts you can enjoy additional returns and cash income from your investments.

VISIONS PIE and other VISIONS investment software tools are available on a free trial basis and can be downloaded at www.RonGroenke.com.

Show Me The Money results for the thirty stocks in the Dow Jones Industrial Index

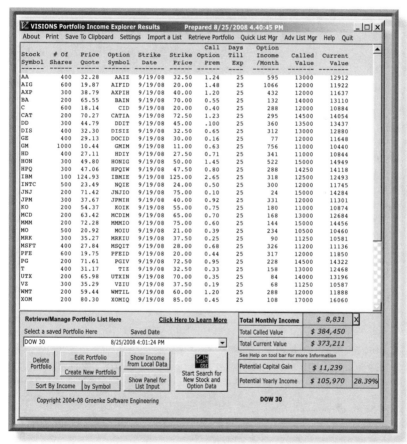

Stock Symbol	# Of Shares	Price Quote	Option Symbol	Strike Date	Strike Price	Call Option Prem	Days Till Exp	Option Income /Month	Called Value	Current Value
AA	400	32.28	AAIZ	9/19/08	32.50	1.24	25	595	13000	12912
AIG	600	19.87	AIFID	9/19/08	20.00	1.48	25	1066	12000	11922
AXP	300	38.79	AXPIH	9/19/08	40.00	1.20	25	432	12000	11637
BA	200	65.55	BAIN	9/19/08	70.00	0.55	25	132	14000	13110
C	600	18.14	CID	9/19/08	20.00	0.40	25	288	12000	10884
CAT	200	70.27	CATIA	9/19/08	72.50	1.23	25	295	14500	14054
DD	300	44.79	DDIT	9/19/08	45.00	.100	25	360	13500	13437
DIS	400	32.30	DISIZ	9/19/08	32.50	0.65	25	312	13000	12880
GE	400	29.13	DOCID	9/19/08	30.00	0.16	25	77	12000	11648
GM	1000	10.44	GMIM	9/19/08	11.00	0.63	25	756	11000	10440
HD	400	27.11	HDIY	9/19/08	27.50	0.71	25	341	11000	10844
HON	300	49.80	HONIG	9/19/08	50.00	1.45	25	522	15000	14949
HPQ	300	47.06	HPQIW	9/19/08	47.50	0.80	25	288	14250	14118
IBM	100	124.93	IBMIE	9/19/08	125.00	2.65	25	318	12500	12493
INTC	500	23.49	NQIE	9/19/08	24.00	0.50	25	300	12000	11745
JNJ	200	71.42	JNJIO	9/19/08	75.00	0.10	25	24	15000	14284
JPM	300	37.67	JPMIH	9/19/08	40.00	0.92	25	331	12000	11301
KO	200	54.37	KOIK	9/19/08	55.00	0.75	25	180	11000	10874
MCD	200	63.42	MCDIM	9/19/08	65.00	0.70	25	168	13000	12684
MMM	200	72.28	MMMIO	9/19/08	75.00	0.60	25	144	15000	14456
MO	500	20.92	MOIU	9/19/08	21.00	0.39	25	234	10500	10460
MRK	300	35.27	MRKIU	9/19/08	37.50	0.25	25	90	11250	10581
MSFT	400	27.84	MSQIT	9/19/08	28.00	0.68	25	326	11200	11136
PFE	600	19.75	PFEID	9/19/08	20.00	0.44	25	317	12000	11850
PG	200	71.61	PGIV	9/19/08	72.50	0.95	25	228	14500	14322
T	400	31.17	TIZ	9/19/08	32.50	0.33	25	158	13000	12468
UTX	200	65.98	UTXIN	9/19/08	70.00	0.35	25	84	14000	13196
VZ	300	35.29	VZIU	9/19/08	37.50	0.19	25	68	11250	10587
WMT	200	59.44	WMTIL	9/19/08	60.00	1.20	25	288	12000	11888
XOM	200	80.30	XOMIQ	9/19/08	85.00	0.45	25	108	17000	16060

Total Monthly Income	$ 8,831	
Total Called Value	$ 384,450	
Total Current Value	$ 373,211	
Potential Capital Gain	$ 11,239	
Potential Yearly Income	$ 105,970	28.39%

DOW 30

Copyright 2004-08 Groenke Software Engineering

These results were provided by the VISIONS Portfolio Income Explorer software program.

Investor Comments

I have been using Ron's VISIONS software and strategy for several years now, and am a believer that "slow and steady" does win the race. My monthly results have averaged out to be about twice the return of the S&P 500. I employ this strategy in several accounts and am seeing a monthly stream of income as a result. Even when negative news about a company results in downside movement in the stock, Ron's strategy limits the loss, and even resulted in a few gains. I'd like to thank Ron for introducing me to the straightforward, low-risk method of generating income with the stock market. I highly recommend *Show Me the Money* to get you started making money on your portfolio.

Bill Datri
Parsippany, NJ

Fifteen years ago a friend and I tried the options market and failed miserably. A year ago I read Ron's book and two comments hit me like a bolt of lightning: 1) You make money by selling, not buying; and, 2) With options, the goal is monthly cash flow, not long term increase in assets. What simple concepts. I'm 72 and don't have time for the long-term. I use Ron's ideas and his VISIONS software and have steadily increased my monthly cash flow.

Javin Taylor
Las Cruces, NM 88007

Ron Groenke started me on a successful and consistent covered call career about one and one-half years back. I will be forever grateful for his kindness and patience. I would urge anyone who is serious about a sustainable income stream with some but very manageable risk to check out Show Me the Money and VISIONS software. They provide an excellent starting point to learning Covered Calls by a master of the trade and one with great teaching skills.

John Spellmann
San Marcos, TX

My Other Books

The Money Tree: Risk Free Options Trading (2002)

*Covered Calls and Naked Puts: Create Your Own
Stock Options Money Tree* (2004)

*Cash For Life: Unlock the Incredible Monthly Cash
Income in Your Stock Portfolio* (2006)

*S*how Me the Money is the fourth in a series of books explaining my "Money Tree" strategy for stock market investing. My strategy is one of repeated singles and doubles . . . not homeruns. Each month I pick a basket of dollars off my stock portfolio by selling Covered Calls and Naked Puts. That monthly cash income grows each month as my portfolio grows.

An important theme in all my books is wise stock selection. After all if you are going to have an orchard of money trees you want the trees to be as healthy as possible. I've created a unique technique for increasing the odds of *buying low and selling higher.*

I've found that the best way to explain my strategy is with a narrative. Beginning with *The Money Tree: Risk Free Options Trading* in 2002 I introduced the story of an average middle age investor who meets his former college finance professor in the small community of Marco Island, Florida. As they renew an old friendship the Professor reveals his secrets for financial success.

My second book in 2004—*Covered Calls and Naked Puts: Create Your Own Stock Options Money Tree*—continued the same theme and narrative with updated examples and more on my Naked Puts strategy.

In 2006, the updated version titled *Cash for Life: Unlock the Incredible Monthly Cash Income in Your Stock Portfolio* was released – The updated version had strategies for ITM (In the Money), OTM (Out of the Money) and ATM (At the Money) and the underpinnings of my technical analysis that is displayed as the VISIONS V. I have published this concept as the Groenke V Theory. Go to **www.RonGroenke.com** and Useful Links for the details.

Show Me the Money: Covered Calls and Naked Puts for a Monthly Cash Income, the latest release, continues the same theme and narrative with important updates and additional strategies.

My books teach you how to earn income in your stock portfolio. They provide the concepts and techniques I have practiced over the past 20 years in generating income on my stock portfolio.

Detailed formulas and stock and option selection criteria are revealed and discussed.

It is my hope that these techniques, which have served me so well, will also be profitable for you.

A word of caution: Be very deliberate in your investing. Do your homework. Study this book carefully and master the techniques. You will find my software, which I call VISIONS Stock Market Explorer to be an important resource. It is the software program that I created and use to find quality stocks. It also shows Call and Put options with premiums that generate the best returns. This software is Internet based and takes the drudgery out of surfing the net for stock and option information. Spend your time analyzing the potential stocks presented by VISIONS. It puts all the information right at your fingertips.

The VISIONS Stock Market Explorer Scout application searches the entire stock market and provides the Top Ten stocks to invest in at the moment. It uses all the fundamentals as discussed in my books and applies technical chart analysis in its stock selection process. Scout has provided investment opportunities that were successful over 80 percent of the time. No one can bat 1000, but these results can put the odds in your favor.

Download a free trial at my website: **www.RonGroenke.com**.

Happy investing,
Ron Groenke

SHOW ME THE MONEY

Covered Calls & Naked Puts
for a Monthly Cash Income

Ronald Groenke

KELLER PUBLISHING
Marco Island, Florida

ISBN 978-I-9340020-8-7

Printed in the United States of America

Published by:

Keller Publishing
590 Fieldstone Dr.
Marco Island, FL 34145

www.KellerPublishing.com

*To my wonderful children
Greg, Steve, and Lori
whom I dearly love.*

Contents

	Acknowledgment	xii
	Disclaimer	xiii
1	As Simple as PIE	1
2	Covered Calls	8
3	Take Control	18
4	Getting Down With the Basics	25
5	The Naked Put	35
6	Riding the Wave	48
7	Build the Prospect List	52
8	Buy Low—Sell High	59
9	A Note of Caution	75
10	The Gift	77
11	Gems and Duds	80
12	Building the Farm Teams	86
13	View from the Top	88
14	When to Take Action	91
15	Show Me the Money	103
16	Despite Taxes and Losses	110
17	Trade Results	124
	Glossary	133
	Appendix A	143
	Appendix B	145
	Appendix C	147
	Investor Comments	171
	Seminar Comments	179

Acknowledgment

Thanks to my friend, Wade Keller, who also is my editor and publisher. After a Rotary Club presentation on my stock options strategy Wade said, "Ron, you've got a book there." That was the beginning of the process that led to this book.

I would also like to acknowledge and give a heartfelt thanks to Wade's wife, Sue, for her interest and friendship.

Disclaimer

There is a high degree of financial risk when trading in the stock and options market. The author and publisher stress that it is possible to lose money that is invested in these markets. The methods and techniques presented in this book may be profitable or they may result in a loss. Past results are not necessarily indicative of future results. The examples of specific companies that are used in this book are only for informational purposes and are not recommendations.

This publication is sold with the understanding that the author and publisher are not engaged in providing legal, accounting, or other professional services. If legal advice or other expert assistance is required, the services of a competent professional should be sought. Although every precaution has been taken in the preparation of this book, the publisher and author assume no liability for errors and omissions. This book is published without warranty of any kind, either expressed or implied. Furthermore, neither the author nor the publisher shall be liable for any damages, either directly or indirectly arising from the use or misuse of the book.

Before investing, learn as much as you can about the investments that you plan to make. Do extensive research. Knowledge will put the odds in your favor.

1

As Simple as PIE

Why not go out on a limb. That's where the fruit is.
Will Rodgers

Jake grimaced. *Not good* he thought as he reached for the thermos, refilled his wife's coffee cup, topped off his own and cleared his throat.

"Katie, we need to talk. This is rather disturbing."

The couple had retired to Marco Island, a resort community off the coast of southwest Florida, after selling their CPA firm in May of the previous year. Somewhere the frantic corporate world of meetings and tax deadlines was in high season. But you couldn't tell it by the Kendall's relaxed schedules. Mornings were spent by the pool on their screened lanai with coffee and bagels. Later they would both be at their computers, Katie doing free-lance stories for the local paper and Jake working on the "Great American Novel."

This morning they had enjoyed an early beach walk and were now side-by-side in their comfortable lounge chairs on the lanai. The morning sun filtered through the large banyan tree and glistened in the pool water. There was worry in Jake's voice and Katie wondered what could possibly have happened in the last few minutes to spoil his happy mood.

Swiveling the screen of his lap top computer so Katie could easily see the matrix, Jake continued.

"Yesterday the market closed up 140 points. But look at our portfolio. Almost all our stocks are down. What the heck are we doing wrong?"

They were both silent for a few moments. Traditionally their savings had been in bank CDs. But after many years of preparing tax returns for all types of investors it had become obvious that stock investments over the long run faired much better than the typically lower yield on CDs. So over the past 20 years they had built a retirement portfolio, which was now their sole source of income. Only a few of their stocks paid dividends. To meet living expenses they would sell sufficient stocks each quarter, hoping—and expecting—that the bulk of the portfolio would continue to grow.

Jake couldn't help but smile as he watched his wife's pursed lips, wrinkled brow and focused concentration on the computer screen. Her dimples were just as cute as when they had first met at the University of Minnesota almost 40 years earlier.

Finally, "Oh Jakey, you know I don't really understand the market. It doesn't seem to make sense, but then how does anyone make sense out of the market. It seems to just be a random process. Maybe we should hire a financial advisor or perhaps buy one of those programs advertised on TV." With a quick smile to Jake she turned back to the community newspaper.

Jake glared at the stock list a few more minutes, then began reading the online edition of the Wall Street Journal. This was his main source of information used to juggle the stocks in their portfolio. He would read about a company that seemed to have good prospects and then sell one of his lagging stocks to get the cash to buy the new stock.

"I'll fix the bagels." Katie hopped up and headed for the kitchen. She soon returned with Jake's favorite: a garlic bagel topped with jalapeno peppers and melted mozzarella cheese.

Taking a bite of her own whole-wheat bagel with cream cheese she asked, "Are you going to Rotary today?"

"Yes. I understand the speaker is some type of stock market guru. Who knows, I might just learn something useful."

***

Jake's eyes feasted on the most beautiful car he had ever seen. A Bentley Continental Flying Spur, it was long and powerful, a statement of roomy elegance. The luxury auto had caught his attention as he was about to enter the Marco Island Yacht Club for the Rotary luncheon. As a long time Rotarian he enjoyed the camaraderie of the group. Several members owned very expensive cars. He was curious, wondering which of his friends had acquired the Bentley.

Taking a seat Jake saw his friend John Scott, the club president, sitting at the head table with the guest speaker, a man who looked strangely familiar. The speaker reminded Jake of a college professor from years ago. What was the name? Graham? Yes, that was it. Professor Robert Graham. But that's not likely he thought. After all, he hadn't seen the professor in over 30 years.

His mind easily slipped back to a particular scene from his college days. He had pulled frantically into the parking lot, already five minutes late for his first class of the semester. It was a warm fall day at the University of Minnesota. Grabbing his books from the back seat he noticed another car jerk to a stop in the vacant slot next to him. Steam was billowing from under the hood and the car was generally banged up. Jake noticed the windshield had a long crack. Apparently the driver's side door wouldn't open because the young man slid across the front seat and quickly out the passenger side with brief case in hand.

"Can I help you?" Jake had asked, concerned that the car might catch on fire.

Noticing Jake for the first time, "Hi. Sorry, don't have time to chat. I'm running late for class. Old Betsy will be OK once she cools off. Powerful thirst." With that he raced into the building.

As Jake made his way to the classroom he was surprised to see the owner of the old clunker standing at the lectern. Finding a seat, Jake noticed the professor had a pleasant smile and twinkle in his eyes as he said to the class, "Welcome to Finance 101. My name is Robert Graham. Don't call me doctor yet as I still have a little work to do on my Ph.D. dissertation. Just call me professor."

"Rotarians please stand!" President Scott sharply banged the gavel against the Rotary bell to begin the meeting, quickly ending Jake's reverie of his college days. The Pledge of Allegiance was followed by invocation and announcements.

"Now, I have the distinct pleasure of introducing our speaker," intoned President Scott. To Jake's amazement it was indeed Robert Graham, Jake's favorite college professor from years ago.

Scott explained that Graham had recently retired to Marco from Minnesota and was now a neighbor in his beachfront condominium. The two men and their wives had become friends and had been out to dinner a few times in the past couple months.

Scott's strong voice filled the room. "Now give a warm Rotary welcome to Dr. Robert Graham."

As Rob Graham accepted the applause and strode to the front of the room, Jake sat up in his chair to get a better look. Something seemed different about the professor. He looked so relaxed and, you might say, prosperous.

"I was a bit reluctant when John invited me to come speak to your Rotary Club," said Graham.

"John wants me to reveal my secret weapon when it comes to making money in the stock market." Graham looked around the room that suddenly became very quiet. Most of the members of the Rotary Club owned stock portfolios and were ready to hear some good news.

"About 18 years ago," Graham continued, "I discovered a way to earn a high rate of return on my stock portfolio and generate monthly income with no additional risk. Yes there is risk in owning stocks. But no additional risk is added to the portfolio by my strategy. As soon as I knew for sure it was working I retired from teaching and devoted all my time to investing. Guess you might say I found a Money Tree.

"Most of you are already thinking that this is some exotic investing scheme and wonder if he will show me the money?

"So the best way to demonstrate my technique is to ask you to name your favorite stocks. Let's build a portfolio of random stocks. President Scott, what's your favorite stock?"

President John Scott was a little surprised to be called on but quickly rose to the occasion. "Well, let's see. I guess one of my favorites is Honeywell."

That got the ball rolling and soon Graham had entered nearly two dozen stocks in his computer. The list was projected on the screen in front of the room for all to see.

"For this show me the money exercise I am going to use a program I call the Portfolio Income Explorer or PIE for short."

Using his Portfolio Income Explorer (PIE) program Graham projected the following table on the screen.

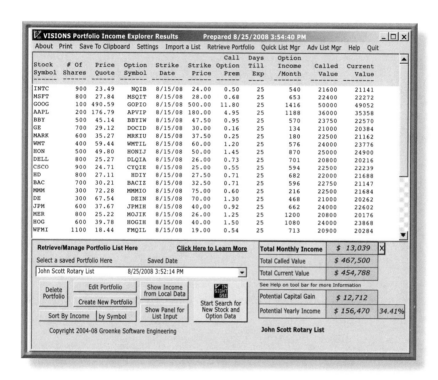

"Using the stocks you gave me I've created a $455,000 portfolio. Rather than just hold the stocks and hope they go up in value, each month I sell Call options. Notice the income of $13,039 per month. If a Call is exercised I have additional capital gain income and can buy additional shares on which to sell Calls. If the Call expires I have the opportunity to sell another Call on the same stock. Either way I'm generating a monthly cash income."

Graham paused and looked around the room. There was an excited buzz from the members. "I've found from many years of teaching that

Q&A is much more effective than lecturing. I'll be glad to take your questions now."

There was appreciative applause as President Scott came back to the front of the room, shook hands with Graham and presented him with a Rotary coffee cup.

"Yes, I agree," began Scott. "Our most effective speakers are short on formal remarks and have better enthusiasm from the audience by responding to questions. This is a rather unruly bunch so I had better field the questions for you."

And indeed the questions came at a fast pace.

What exactly is a stock option? I thought you could only buy options. I didn't know you could sell them. Can an average investor actually sell options? What size portfolio is this plan effective? How about with an IRA? What about Puts? Do you sell Puts too? How do you pick good stocks? Do you use a discount broker? Which one?

At 1 pm sharp, President Scott rang the bell again, this time to signal the meeting was adjourned. At least a dozen members crowded around and continued to ask questions. Jake waited patiently and was finally able to introduce himself to the professor as they were walking out.

"Hi professor. Remember me? Jake Kimball. I was in your finance class at U of M, fall of 1970."

Rob shook hands and smiled as he searched his memory bank. So many students over a twenty-year teaching career. And now he had been retired from teaching for eighteen years.

"Hmmm. You say you were in my class at the University of Minnesota. That was actually my first teaching job. Wait a minute. Were you by chance that enterprising student who helped me get my car started after my first class? You had something you poured in the radiator to stop the leak. And then we used a bucket to get water and fill up the radiator."

Jake was smiling and nodding. "Yes, that was me. It was a good class, Finance 101, but as an Accounting major I only needed the one finance class."

They continued talking as they walked out to the parking lot. Jake noticed they were heading in the direction of the Bentley he had admired earlier. His first thought was serious doubt that a former college professor could own such an expensive car. But, nevertheless they were soon standing next to the Continental Flying Spur. Jake's look of amazement was obvious.

Rob smiled and said, "This is Old Betsy. A little different from the one you helped me with."

"Wow! Look professor, I think I need to know more about your investment strategy. I mean, I think I understood most of your presentation in the meeting. But I've got a lot of questions. I've heard of Calls and Puts, but I always thought they were rather exotic—and risky. But, you are apparently using them to create monthly income. And that's just what I've been trying to do with my portfolio, except what I do is sell stocks to get cash to pay bills. But you've got another way. How can I learn to do what you are doing?"

Rob had actually missed teaching since turning full time to investing. Seeing his students have an "Ah Hah!" experience was personally rewarding.

"Hmmm. Maybe it is about time I became a professor again." Rob was already pulling out his PDA and punching a number. "Let me make a quick call."

"Hello Jean. I'm going to be about 30 minutes late. I met an old friend at the Rotary meeting. See you at home. Yes love. I love you too."

Then he reached in the Bentley and retrieved a notebook. "I have an example in here. Let's go back inside and sit down at a table."

Tiffany, the hostess, greeted them with a warm smile and escorted them to a secluded table when they explained their purpose. "You won't be disturbed here," she said. "Can I bring you tea or coffee?"

Moments later Jake was feeling a sense of high anticipation. He squeezed a lemon in his ice tea and waited. Finally, Rob pulled a single sheet of paper out of his notebook, looked at the paper and looked at Jake. Then he slid the sheet of paper across the table.

2

Covered Calls

A genius is a talented person who does his homework.
Thomas A. Edison

"Jake, what I am showing you is very simple and yet very power-ful," said Graham.

"This is an investment I made in Interdigital Communications. IDCC is one of the leading companies that provide technology for wireless communications. If you use a cell phone, one of their integrated circuits may be inside. Study the chart carefully and tell me what you see."

INTERDIGITAL COMMUNICATIONS				IDCC	DAQ	MAR JUN	SEP DEC	
11-24-03	B		1000		20.29	20295.00	-20295.00	
11-24-03	S	10	DEC	20.00	1.30	1279.93	-19015.07	CE
12-22-03	S	10	MAR	20.00	2.35	2329.89	-16685.18	CE
03-22-04	S	10	JUN	20.00	.65	629.97	-16055.21	CE
06-21-04	S	10	SEP	20.00	.95	929.97	-15125.24	CE
09-20-04	S	10	JAN	20.00	.75	729.98	-14395.26	CE
01-24-05	S	10	MAR	20.00	1.00	979.96	-13415.30	CE
03-21-05	S	10	JUN	20.00	.90	794.92	-12620.38	CE
06-20-05	S	10	AUG	20.00	1.15	1129.95	-11490.43	CE
08-22-05	S	10	DEC	20.00	1.00	979.95	-10510.48	CE
12-19-05	S	10	MAR	20.00	.70	684.97	-9825.51	CA
03-17-06	C		1000		20.00	19980.00	10154.49	<

Jake took a few minutes to study the chart. "Professor, I believe I understand part of the first line. On November 24, 2003 you bought 1000 shares of IDCC at $20.29 a share. But, I'm not sure I understand the last three columns. Where did the 20295.00 come from? And why do the numbers in the second to last column go from negative to positive?"

"This is my short hand way of keeping up with my investments," explained Graham.

"I've given this a lot of thought and have developed my own software program that analyzes each of my investments as part of my overall portfolio. My primary concern is cash flow. I don't like to lose money. On each investment my first objective is to have a positive cash flow. My second objective is to have a very positive cash flow. We'll talk more about monthly income later. First, let's make sure you understand the basics here.

"You are correct that I bought 1000 shares of IDCC. The price per share was $20.29. I use a discount, on-line broker and the sales commission was $5.00. Add the sales commission of $5.00 to the purchase of 1000 shares at $20.29 a share and you have my total cash outflow. For this one purchase my total cash outflow was $20,295.00. The third to last column is the transaction amount and the second to last column is a running total or the cumulative effect of all the transactions. Since this was a cash outflow the dollar amount is shown as a negative.

"But, now let's take a look at the second line of the IDCC chart. On the same day that I bought the 1000 shares, I sold 10 contracts of December Calls at a strike price of $20.00. The S in the second column means I made a sale. In the next three columns the "10 DEC 20.00" tells me what I sold. One contract is for 100 shares, the minimum needed to sell an option. So my 1000 shares of stock allow me to sell 10 contracts. That means that at the time the market price of IDCC was $20.29 a share I sold the option for someone to buy my 1000 shares for $20.00 a share any time up until the close of the market on the third Friday the following December.

"So the 10 in column three represents the number of contracts, 10 contracts or 1000 shares. DEC, in column four, is the month of

expiration. The expiration date is always the third Friday, so just des-
ignating the month is sufficient. The 20.00 in column five is the strike
price. The strike price is a critical figure because it determines whether
or not the Call option will expire or be exercised. If the market price
drifts at or below $20.00 it will not be profitable for the buyer of the
option to buy my shares for $20.00. If the market price is above $20.00
it will be profitable for the option buyer to exercise the option.

"Now look at column six. This is the cash I earned by selling the
option. The price I received for that option was $1.30 per share. Less
the commission, that came to $1279.93, which is shown in the next
column, abbreviated as 1279.93. Notice that the transaction amount,
$1,279.93 in this case, is positive. Selling the Call means I received
money, so it is a cash inflow. That has the effect of reducing the
cumulative balance in the next to last column. At this point my net
investment is $19,015.07 for the 1000 shares of IDCC. That's the net
of the cost of the investment, $20,295.00, and the option income
I immediately earned, $1,279.93. The broker commission, $20.07
($1300.00 less $1279.93) was a little higher on the sale of the option
than the purchase of the stock. But they are both fairly small when
you use a discount broker.

"My strategy here is called a Covered Call. I owned 1000 shares of
IDCC stock, and on those shares I sold a Call option. It's called a "covered" Call because, in the event the stock is called, I'm already covered.
I already own the stock and can readily hand it over. The purchaser of
the option has the right, but not the obligation, to purchase my 1000
shares for $20.00 a share anytime up to the close of the market on
December 19, 2003, which was the third Friday in December that year.
Options always expire on the 3rd Friday. I received the premium of
$1,279.93 for selling that right or option. Now the purchaser can be
expected to exercise the option if the market price of IDCC is above
$20.00 during that time period. It could be exercised anytime before
expiration, but most likely the option would not be exercised until the
last day of the option period. Of course it would be foolish to exercise
the option if the market price is below $20. If the market price were
below $20, one could buy cheaper in the market rather then buying
my stock for $20.

"As it turned out the Call option was not exercised. See the "CE" at the end of line two. CE stands for "Call Expired." My 1000 shares of IDCC are no longer committed."

Jake was beginning to see an entirely new concept in stock ownership. "Hmmmm, you are actually generating a monthly stream of income just from owning stocks. This is just what I need. Do many people do this? Are there many stocks that you can do this with? I am still wondering what kind of investment return can you make?"

"Hold on Jake. First let me ask you a few questions. Maybe it would be best if you told me your impression of the stock market." Graham's professorial techniques were kicking in.

Jake thought for a moment before responding.

"Individual stocks go up and down. Over time most of the stocks go up more than they go down so the overall market goes up gradually over time. The market is always somewhat risky because some stocks go down more than up and may even end up worthless. We have our investments diversified in about 15 stocks."

Jake continued, "As for options, I've always heard of people buying options and that it is a gamble. You are hoping the stock will shoot up. If it does you make a lot of money. But, if it doesn't, you just lose your investment. It becomes worthless as the option period runs out. I always thought of that as gambling, like playing blackjack in Vegas. It never occurred to me that people actually sell options."

Graham nodded. "That's a pretty good analysis of the market Jake. You're right, a lot of people buy stock options hoping the underlying stock will shoot up. But, it is much more likely that the stock will move in a narrow range in a short period of time. My motto is ***You make money by selling, not by buying.***

"Here's my PDA." Graham pushed a button to turn one side of the PDA to a touch screen calculator. "For your first test this semester, what was my return on investment from selling those ten contracts on November 24, 2003? By the way, one contract is 100 shares of stock."

Jake eagerly began analyzing the data and solving the problem. He decided that the return for selling the Call was $1,279.93. Now what should be the investment base to divide into the return? Well, apparently the total cash outflow of $20,295.00. Dividing the former by the later he got 6.31%. He started to state the answer but then the thought occurred: over what time period? Sure, 6.31%was a good return, but that was for less than a year. What was the APR, annual percentage rate? How many days from November 24, 2003 to December 19, 2003? He recalled the procedure: Subtract 24 from 30 and add 19. A quick count gave him 25 days. So to annualize the return he multiplied 6.31% by 365 and divided by 25.

Looking at the professor he said with a smile, "92.126%. That is just amazing."

"Jake, that's good. Actually, I never bother to annualize. I have another technique that I'll tell you about later. I'm satisfied with a good, quick return. Just for the heck of it compute the return for line three."

Jake quickly noted that the premium per share for the next sell of ten Call contracts was $2.35 per share. After commissions Rob had netted $2,329.89. Now what was the amount of investment at that time? Presumably it is $19,015.07. He quickly made the computation.

"I get 12.25% without annualizing. However, annualizing would be fairly simple. It took three months to earn the 12.25%. So just quadruple it for the APR. Either way it's a darn good return."

Jake was beginning to get the hang of it. "The CE on the end of your net investment on line three means the Call expired, so you were able to do it again. I'll compute the gain on line four. Let's see. You again sold 10 contacts, this time at $.65 per share. After commissions you netted $629.97. By the way, Professor, when do you get this money?"

"It goes immediately into my brokerage account. I can take it out and spend it or I can invest it. The choice is mine. I earned it by selling the option."

Jake was amazed as the concept sunk in. "So this really is new money. You have earned money on your portfolio but it's not capital gains and it's not dividends. I had no idea you could do this."

Graham smiled. He always enjoyed seeing the light come on with his students when he explained a new financial concept.

"Very good. Now here's another question for you. Most investment advisors say the way to make money in the stock market is to buy good stocks and hold for long-term appreciation. How much of my return on IDCC was a result of stock appreciation or dividends?"

Jake cautiously considered the question. He looked closely at the chart again.

INTERDIGITAL COMMUNICATIONS IDCC	DAQ	MAR	JUN	SEP	DEC			
11-24-03	B		1000		20.29	20295.00	-20295.00	
11-24-03	S	10	DEC	20.00	1.30	1279.93	-19015.07	CE
12-22-03	S	10	MAR	20.00	2.35	2329.89	-16685.18	CE
03-22-04	S	10	JUN	20.00	.65	629.97	-16055.21	CE
06-21-04	S	10	SEP	20.00	.95	929.97	-15125.24	CE
09-20-04	S	10	JAN	20.00	.75	729.98	-14395.26	CE
01-24-05	S	10	MAR	20.00	1.00	979.96	-13415.30	CE
03-21-05	S	10	JUN	20.00	.90	794.92	-12620.38	CE
06-20-05	S	10	AUG	20.00	1.15	1129.95	-11490.43	CE
08-22-05	S	10	DEC	20.00	1.00	979.95	-10510.48	CE
12-19-05	S	10	MAR	20.00	.70	684.97	-9825.51	CA
03-17-06	C		1000		20.00	19980.00	10154.49	<

"Professor, you told me that CE stands for Call Expired. There are nine CE's and then a CA. What does CA stand for?"

"CA stands for Call Assigned. Notice the second to last column of the second to last line is -9825.51 followed by CA. That means that the Call sold on December 19, 2005 was assigned. The owners of the Call option exercised their right to buy my 1000 shares of stock for $20 a share. That's shown on the last line with a C in the second column. See the positive cash flow of $19,980.00. That's the proceeds from the sale, 1,000 shares times $20 per share less $20 brokerage fee.

"You can see by the balance in the second to last column that my profit for this investment was $10,154.49. So now you should be able to tell me how much of my profit is from stock appreciation or dividends."

"To help you remember what the CA, CE, etc. stand for here is a card with the definitions. Keep this handy as you study the example."

Transaction Definitions

Code after date
P = Plan (date is in the future)
B = Buy
S = Sell
C = Called

Code at end of transaction
CA = Call Assigned
CE = Call Expired
CO = Call Open (date is in the future)
CC = Call Closed (option was bought back)

PA = Put Assigned
PE = Put Expired
PO = Put Open (date is in the future)
PC = Put Closed (option was bought back)

< = All positions have closed (ie. the buy and sell cycle has completed).

Jake took the card and thought for another moment as he analyzed the chart. Finally, he said, "You bought the 1000 shares for $20.29 each and are willing to sell them for $20 each. That's a twenty-nine cent per share loss. All of your return was from selling Call options ten times. Apparently none of your return was from dividends. I would say you made nothing from stock appreciation. But there was a profit of $10,154.49 when your stock was called. We have 10154.49 divided by 20295.00, which is 50.03% in roughly 28 months or 21.44% per year."

"That's right," said Graham. "Think of it as picking money from a money tree like you would pick fruit from an orchard. I tend to do short term option sales, pick some dollars and hope to get called. I never mind if the stock shoots up and the option buyer makes a profit. Usually the option expires and I can pick some more money from the same tree. In this example, I picked cash ten times from this one money tree. The cash flowed into my monthly income account. I'm satisfied with a good return every few months."

As the professor began to gather his papers Jake was thinking fast.

"But wait a minute," Jake questioned. "There has to be a catch. This is too good to be true. What if you are picking fruit as the price of the stock is headed down?"

"Good point. And that can happen. In fact, I think I have another example here that illustrates just that experience." Graham pulled a sheet of paper out of his notebook and handed it to Jake. "Cott Corporation is a soft drink bottler. You can see that its stock price went from $9.50 a share down to $3.81 a share. During that time I picked so much fruit from the tree I made a profit of $9,847.80 even though I finally sold the stock at a substantial loss.

"As I said before, there is a definite risk in owning stock, but that risk can be greatly mitigated, and in some cases even overcome, by selling Calls. This particular investment reminds me of a small town in Minnesota. Have you ever heard of Andover?"

Jake was still analyzing the sheet of paper detailing Graham's investment in Cott. He was counting the number of times Calls had been sold on this single investment. He mumbled, "No, don't think so."

COTT CORPORATION					COTTF	CQT FEB MAY AUG	NOV
11-08-94	B		1500		9.5000	14279.00	-14279.00	
11-08-94	S	15	MAY	10.00	1.5625	2298.67	-11980.33	CE
11-30-94	B		1500		10.0000	15029.00	-27009.33	
11-30-94	S	15	MAY	10.00	1.7500	2579.91	-24429.42	CE
05-22-95	S	30	NOV	10.00	.9375	2742.40	-21687.02	CE
02-09-95	B		2000		9.6200	19279.00	-40966.02	
02-09-95	S	20	AUG	10.00	1.3750	2694.90	-38271.12	CE
08-22-95	S	20	NOV	10.00	.6250	1199.95	-37071.17	CE
11-15-95	S	50	MAY	10.00	.6250	3024.89	-34046.28	CE
05-20-96	S	50	NOV	10.00	.7500	3649.87	-30396.41	CE
11-18-96	S	50	MAY	10.00	.4375	2087.42	-28308.99	CE
05-19-97	S	50	AUG	10.00	.6250	3024.89	-25284.10	CE
08-18-97	S	20	NOV	10.00	.6250	1199.95	-24084.15	CE
08-18-97	S	30	NOV	10.00	.5625	1637.44	-22446.71	CE
11-24-97	S	50	FEB	10.00	.7500	3649.87	-18796.84	CE
02-24-98	S	50	MAY	10.00	.6250	3024.89	-15771.95	CE
05-15-98	S	50	AUG	7.50	.5000	2397.41	-13374.54	CE
08-25-98	S	50	NOV	7.50	.5000	2397.41	-10977.13	CE
11-17-98	S	50	MAY	7.50	.3750	1772.43	-9204.70	CE
06-23-99	S		5000		3.8100	19052.50	9847.80	<

"The story, perhaps mythical, of how the town got its name is interesting. As the story goes, the Great Northern Railroad had a stop at a small northern community. One morning there was a derailment and the train rolled over and over and over. This accident was such a big news story the residents decided to rename the town Andover, to capture the event forever in history. I'm reminded of the name, Andover, when I sell Calls over and over."

Just then Tiffany arrived with two slices of cherry pie and refills for their tea. "On the house guys. It's fresh today but won't keep until tomorrow. And we are closing in fifteen minutes."

"Thanks Tiffany," said Jake. "I guess we had better wrap this up. My head is pounding with all this new information."

"You've learned a lot in one day," agreed Rob. "Now to be sure you really understand let me give you a simple homework assignment.

"Get a copy of Investors Business Daily or the Wall Street Journal. Go to the options page and pick three stocks that you are familiar with. I want you to assume a purchase of 100 shares of each stock and the sale of one Covered Call contract.

"This will be just on paper so you get familiar with how it works. For each stock pick four different possible options. The options will vary based on strike price and expiration date. So for each stock you might have one option that expires in one month and has a strike price more that market price, another that expires in three months and has a strike price less than market price, and so forth. Do you see what I mean?

"Yes," replied Jake. "I can see that this will be an important exercise to understand how to make money selling options. I am still just amazed that I was never even aware of this possibility."

"Don't worry about that. You are not alone. Most investors are not aware of the untapped profits in their portfolios. Remember, once you've bought the stock you have assumed the risk of stock ownership. What you're doing by selling Calls is generating income by what I refer to as picking dollars off the money tree.

"You will find option prices for both Calls and Puts. For now, just concentrate on Calls. I will explain my strategy with Puts later.

"Do you recall the IDCC option that I sold on November 24, 2003 that you were analyzing earlier? Remember how it was designated.

16

It reads 10 DEC 20.00. That means the strike price is $20 for the 10 contracts. Options expire on the third Friday of each month. Since this is a December option in 2003, the expiration date is December 19. In considering an option for my IDCC stock I selected DEC 20.00. Others that I considered were DEC 22.50, MAR 20.00, and MAR 22.50. As I said before, options vary based on strike price and expiration date.

"Once you've selected four different options for each stock, compute the return for each of the four contracts assuming first CE (the Call expires) and then CA (the Call is assigned). Those are the only two things that can happen. The Call will expire, CE, or the Call will be assigned, CA. Compute your return both ways. You will be making a total of 12 computations, four for each of the three stocks.

"You had better write down the formulas for computing the return. They are:

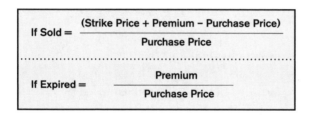

$$\text{If Sold} = \frac{(\text{Strike Price} + \text{Premium} - \text{Purchase Price})}{\text{Purchase Price}}$$

$$\text{If Expired} = \frac{\text{Premium}}{\text{Purchase Price}}$$

"You'll be surprised how much you learn just doing this exercise."

Jake was writing furiously on the sheet of paper. Seeing that his student was getting the big picture the professor smiled.

Taking a last bite of cherry pie he said, "You will never look at your stock portfolio the same again. Now you see why I refer to this process as *picking dollars off the money tree.*

3

Take Control

Failure is the opportunity to begin again, more intelligently.
Henry Ford

"Katie my love, you are not going to believe who I met at Rotary today." Jake arrived home in a state of excitement with his newly purchased copy of the Wall Street Journal.

"Let me guess," replied Katie with a sly smile. "Could it possibly have been Rob Graham, the Finance Professor you had in college?" As Jake's mouth hung open she continued.

"I've just been on the phone with Candy. She covers the Rotary Club events for the Sun Times. It's a small island Jakey. Not much happens here without my knowing about it. And by the way, Lori and Steve are back from their cruise and would like for us to come over for cocktails and sunset on their balcony. So I accepted. Is that alright?"

"Sure. You know I'm always glad to visit with Steve and Lori. Besides I need to pick Steve's brain. He retired near the top of that big brokerage firm. With all the money they have he must have done really well as a stockbroker, or analyst, whatever he was. But right now I've got homework to do. I'm computing how much money we can make by selling Covered Calls."

"Covered who? Oh, never mind. Just let me know when I can read another chapter of your novel. I'm anxious to find out how your "Walter Mitty" CPA character saves the nation from financial ruin."

18

As Jake did his computations he became increasingly familiar with the operations of the options market. Several points became obvious. Apparently there were three factors in his decision process, which determined the amount of premium he could receive by selling a Call option.

First, the time period to the expiration date was important. He considered two options based on the same stock and with the same strike price but different expiration months. The premiums differed and that was to be expected. Obviously the longer the option period the more opportunity for a stock to shoot up in value. So the option buyer would pay more for a longer option period. But then he noticed a more subtle distinction. There was not a direct correlation between time and value. A three-month option, while more than a one-month option, was not three times greater. The time value of money had a slight offsetting effect to the time value of options. Jake wondered if the professor's strategy somehow took that into account.

The second factor under his control was the selection of the strike price. If a stock were selling for $12.50, a strike price of $15 would pay less than a strike price of $10. That made sense because with a $15 strike price the stock price would have to rise more than $2.50 before the option would be exercised. A strike price of $10 meant the stock was already $2.50 above the price at which it could be bought by the option holder. The $10 strike price meant the option already had $2.50 of intrinsic value in addition to its time value.

This was an important consideration. The premium one could receive for selling a Call would always have time value and might also have intrinsic value. One of the stocks Jake selected for his pretend purchase had a market value of $17. He considered a June 15 option. That meant that the purchaser of Jake's option could buy the stock for $15 anytime up until the third Friday in June, about a month off. The premium was $2.50. Jake could receive $2.50 per share by selling the option. $2.00 of the $2.50 was intrinsic value—the difference between the $17 market price and the $15 strike price. The remaining 50 cents per share was for the possibility that the stock would rise in value more than 50 cents in the next month. So, the premium consisted of intrinsic value plus time value.

On the same $17 stock Jake considered a June 20 option. That meant that the buyer of the option could buy the stock for $20 up until the third Friday in June. That option premium was only 30 cents per share—no intrinsic value and only a small time value.

The third factor affecting the amount of the premium was the particular stock that he selected. Jake found two stocks that had the same closing market price the previous day. When he checked the option premium for each, using the same strike price and expiration date, he found that stock A would yield a significantly higher premium than stock B. Maybe that had something to do with the volatility of the stock.

That would bear checking out.

He began to formulate some questions for the professor. First, how do you know which stocks to buy? Is it just random or is there a way to wisely select stocks? Second, for a given stock, how do you know which of the various options with different strike prices and time periods to choose? He began to suspect that once he had those questions answered there would be more questions. Also, what was the deal with Puts? He noticed that the stocks had both Put and Call options. Jake was deep in thought when Katie came over and pulled on his ear lobe.

"Let's go for a walk, handsome, and you can tell me how much money we are going to make with that covered stuff. We'll need to get back in plenty of time to make sunset with Steve and Lori."

***

"Jake, I'm telling you. You have got to go on one of these world cruises. Around the world in 80 days. Every few days you are in a new port."

Steve Peterson dipped a shrimp in the special sauce Lori had prepared. "So, tell me what's been going on here while we've been gone. Anything exciting?"

Jake and Katie had enjoyed a vigorous walk on the beach, showered and changed before going to the Peterson's penthouse condo for sunset and cocktails. Steve was in his usual bombastic mood. He had already extolled the virtues of his favorite sports teams and denigrated the lack of virtue of certain local political figures.

"Yes," Jake replied. "You missed Rotary today. Our speaker was Rob Graham. He was my Finance Professor over thirty years ago. I recognized him almost right away. He had a certain presence in the classroom, you might say charisma, that makes him easy to remember."

Lori came out to offer margarita refills. Jake mused, "Lori, you are always so philosophical. Isn't it rather interesting that I should meet my old professor after all these years? How could that be?"

Lori smiled impishly as she refilled glasses. "When the student is ready, the teacher will appear. But, most of all, be what you want, but always be you." She winked at her husband as she turned to join Katie back inside.

Steve was not one to spend too much time pondering his wife's words of wisdom. "You'll notice," he continued with enthusiasm, because this was his favorite time of day, "that the bottom of the sun has just touched the Gulf of Mexico. It will be exactly two minutes and forty six seconds until the sun is completely down. And I would say the conditions are good for a green flash this evening. Humidity is low and there are only a few clouds near the horizon."

The green flash was a popular topic of conversation. It occurred rarely and would only happen when the last of the sun dipped into the sea. Perhaps one time in a hundred a green flash could be seen just at that moment of last sunlight. You could consider yourself lucky if you saw it once. But of course the Petersons had seen it numerous times with their front row seat.

"Speaking of green," Jake piped in, "what do you think of making money in the options market?"

"You will lose your shirt!" Steve replied with conviction. "You might as well go to Vegas and play the craps table. In my thirty years on Wall Street I never knew anyone to consistently make money buying options. It's just a gamble."

"Steve, I never did understand exactly what you did on Wall Street."

"I started off as a broker. And then I managed one of our branch offices with about 50 brokers. So, we were basically in sales. I would have clients occasionally who would insist on playing the options market. After they lost all they could afford, I would then get them into some good solid companies for long-term growth. I tell you, people who think they can manage their own money in the stock market, why that's like trying to operate on yourself. There are some things that just need to be handled by professionals, and the stock market is one of them. My clients over the years would just turn every thing over to me. They didn't want to be bothered with the decisions. And of course, my job was to preserve their capital. I guess you could say my motto was *Preserve and Grow Slowly.* And it paid off. We've been retired for fifteen years now, enjoying the good life."

A lone pelican glided by on the way to hopefully catch a snack in the gulf. Steve paused just long enough to admire the pelican's head-long dive into the water.

"Options traders think they can predict the future. They think they can pick a stock that will definitely go up in value. So to increase the return they buy options on that destined-to-rise stock. But I say no wise man has ever wished to see what the future holds."

"Wait a minute Steve. That sounds pretty good. Maybe you should share it with Lori, the philosopher. How did it go? No wise man has ever wished to see what the future holds?"

Steve was not entirely sure that Jake wasn't being a little sarcastic. He continued, "In life, as in stock investments, be willing to be pleasantly surprised no matter what comes your way. Don't risk being hung out to dry by heavy gambles in the options market."

Steve waxed on, "You know the old 80–20 rule. It's formally called the Pareto Principle after the Italian economist who discovered that generally 80% of the wealth was owned by 20% of the people. But it applies to a lot more than just wealth distribution. For example 80% of my problems came from the 20% of my clients who were always coming up with a hot stock tip or strategy, like the ones who wanted to gamble in the options market. I would give those clients to new trainees and keep the satisfied clients. All brokers prefer clients who appreciate their knowledge and expertise. Leave the driving to us, so to speak."

Steve leaned back in the lounge chair and smiled contentedly, enjoying the warm breeze, commanding view of the beach and the gulf. Four more pelicans gracefully flew by. There were sailboats in the distance. The clouds were just right to pick up a red tint from the sun.

Jake had listened and waited patiently. Waited to ask the one key question. He turned to look directly at Steve.

"But what if, Steve, instead of buying options, you sold options. And suppose further that you only sold options on stock that you already owned. Would that not be risk free income?"

Steve was about to take a sip of his margarita, Lori's specialty. Lori liked to brag that she had learned the secret recipe after chatting with the bartender at a local Mexican restaurant. The glass had reached Steve's lips and seemed to be frozen there. Time stood still. Finally Steve set the glass down and absentmindedly licked the salt off his lips. His voice was usually a little on the loud side. But now it was low, just barely audible. He seemed almost to be talking to himself.

"Hmmm. Sell options on stock that you own. Yes that would seem to work. Maybe that's why so many people buying options lose money. It's because people selling options are making money. If the stock goes up above the strike price you sell at a profit. You get the premium and part of the stock appreciation. If the stock goes down you still keep the premium. Psychologically you are not that concerned that the stock go up right away. Long term sure you want it to go up and, if you pick a good stock, it will. But if the stock goes down you could buy the option back for pennies on the dollar and sell it again when the stock goes back up. Or just wait for the option to expire and then sell a new contract on the same stock. What's the risk? Well the stock price could move up sharply and your gain on the up side would be limited. But that rarely happens. Stocks move up over time but over short periods like three months, they mostly just move up and down within a narrow range. And if the stock goes up you would have to sell in order to realize the gain. Most investors just hold on to the stock expecting it to go higher, as it drifts back down to equilibrium level. Of course the real risk is that the stock could go down. But you have that risk whether you sell options or not. So if you mean by 'risk free income' no additional risk then . . . ."

Steve interrupted his rambling monologue and shouted to Lori, "Honey, would you bring me the Investors Business Daily." And then to Jake, "I wonder what kind of premium I could get on my portfolio? Why you know the more I think about it the more obvious it is. Hardly any stocks pay a decent dividend any more. The portfolio is just sitting there. And I'm sitting here hoping the market will go up a little bit. I've got dozens of stocks that have been virtually flat over the past couple of years. Might as well generate a little income while they're sitting there. Jake, let me fix you another drink. Lori, did you throw out the papers?"

Jake noticed that the sky had become even more beautiful after the sunset. An osprey had caught a fish and was flying back to the nest. Jake smiled, looking forward to his next meeting with the professor.

4

Getting Down
With the Basics

*If you are given a choice between money and sex appeal, take the
money. As you get older, the money will become your sex appeal.*
Katherine Hepburn, at age 87

Tiffany smiled when she saw Rob and Jake headed her way. "What
are you guys doing here today? Rotary's not until Thursday." Tiffany had run on the college track team with Jake's daughter and fell
in love with Marco Island while visiting on spring break. She and
Jake were good friends and always kidded each other. Sometimes she
would affectionately call him Uncle Jake.

"Urgent business Tiff," Jake responded. "I'm learning how to plant a
money tree. And if you give us good service I may show you how to
plant one too." At Jake's request Rob had agreed to meet on Monday
afternoon for a spot of tea and another investment lesson.

Tiffany seated them at a secluded table and went for the tea. Jake
opened a folder in which he had his homework assignment and a
series of questions.

"Professor, I hardly know where to start. Over the past 20 years I've
generally invested any surplus funds in the market. Katie and I built
our retirement fund that way. But it's always been a straight investment and I generally just relied on the advice of my stockbroker or

a hot tip I got from a client. And I made regular contributions to a mutual fund IRA. Now, after our discussion last week and the homework assignment, I see a whole new possibility for earning income on a stock portfolio. I guess my key question is how to select stocks. Is it just random or is there a way to improve the odds. And also, while I now have some understanding of selling Calls, I don't have a clue about Puts. Are Puts part of the money tree? And there's the matter of . . ."

"Jake, hold on." Rob grinned as Tiffany poured hot water on the herbal tea bag in each cup. "One step at a time."

Tiffany teasingly gave Jake a pat on the head as she said, "I overheard part of what you two were talking about last week." Turning to Rob and holding out her hand she said, "By the way, I'm Tiffany. Welcome to Marco Island."

"Thank you Tiffany. The hospitality is great and the weather is terrific. Are you interested in investments?"

"Oh yes. I joined an investment club. We're members of NAIC which stands for National Association of Investors Corporation. There are 20 of us pooling $50 a week. So far at our meetings no one has mentioned options. I wonder if you would be willing to make a presentation."

Just then two couples entered the restaurant. "Got to go. I'll be back," as she bustled off.

"She's a great kid," Jake commented. "And a real hustler. I've never seen a young person with such eclectic interests. She coaches young girls at the Y in volleyball and basketball and frequently is in plays produced by Marco Players, our community theater group. And now, by golly, she's interested in investments."

"But professor," Jake continued. "Where do we go from here? I want to learn it all. But, I know what you said is important. 'One step at a time'."

"Yes, that's right," agreed Rob. "What we need to do right now is be sure you have the basics down. Let's take a look at one of your homework assignments."

"OK. That's good because that brings up one of my key questions. Here's an analysis I did on Calls available on Wal-Mart. I know you said to get four options for each stock, but on this one I computed the return on six. I used your shorthand CA for Call Assigned and CE for Call Expired."

WalMart—WMT Date: May 23, 2008 Stock price 55.75			
Month/Strike	Bid	% If CA	% If CE
Jul 55.00	2.43	3.01	4.35
Jul 57.50	1.20	5.29	2.15
Sep 55.00	3.55	5.02	6.36
Sep 57.50	2.28	7.22	4.08
Dec 55.00	4.70	7.08	8.43
Dec 57.50	3.45	9.32	6.18

"It was easy enough to get the data. That was readily available. And computing the percentages was easy using the formulas from our last session. But how do I make a judgment as to the best month and strike price?"

Rob smiled. "WalMart. Interesting company. I have used WMT for a few of my trades the past few years. Seems to have very modest movements but is now at the same price it was six years ago. That has not helped all of the folks who have bought and held. It serves as a good example of how you can beat the pants off the return on a CD with a fairly stable, conservative stock. Notice the 7.08% and 8.43% returns for DEC 55. And that's for less than 7 months. Try getting that on a CD.

"So which option should you select? You need my Magic Chart. I have one here in my folder.

"Selecting the best premium for a Covered Call plagued me for the first couple of years I was selling options. This area is mostly science and a little art. The goal in selling Calls is to generate a number of small gains on a continuous basis. If you want a larger premium, the time factor will be longer. ***Time IS Money in this case.*** How do we strike a balance between time and the overall gain? Through experience on simulating multiple option cycles, and allowing for losses, I developed the following rate of return table for option premiums. Find the current month in the top row and the expiration month in the body of the table. Guided by the Magic Chart I've successfully generated an average gain of 25% or more per year over a ten-year period."

Rob handed Jake the chart the size of an index card with calculations on the front and back. One side was for the months January through June. The other side had the months July through December.

THE MAGIC CHART – SIDE ONE

MONTHS TO EXP.	IF SOLD	IF EXP.	JAN	FEB	MAR	APR	MAY	JUN
1	6.8	5.4	FEB	MAR	APR	MAY	JUN	JUL
2	8.4	6.7	MAR	APR	MAY	JUN	JUL	AUG
3	10.0	8.0	APR	MAY	JUN	JUL	AUG	SEP
4	11.6	9.3	MAY	JUN	JUL	AUG	SEP	OCT
5	13.4	10.7	JUN	JUL	AUG	SEP	OCT	NOV
6	15.0	12.0	JUL	AUG	SEP	OCT	NOV	DEC
7	16.6	13.3	AUG	SEP	OCT	NOV	DEC	JAN
8	18.4	14.7	SEP	OCT	NOV	DEC	JAN	FEB
9	20.0	16.0	OCT	NOV	DEC	JAN	FEB	MAR

THE MAGIC CHART – SIDE TWO

MONTHS TO EXP.	IF SOLD	IF EXP.	JUL	AUG	SEP	OCT	NOV	DEC
1	6.8	5.4	AUG	SEP	OCT	NOV	DEC	JAN
2	8.4	6.7	SEP	OCT	NOV	DEC	JAN	FEB
3	10.0	8.0	OCT	NOV	DEC	JAN	FEB	MAR
4	11.6	9.3	NOV	DEC	JAN	FEB	MAR	APR
5	13.4	10.7	DEC	JAN	FEB	MAR	APR	MAY
6	15.0	12.0	JAN	FEB	MAR	APR	MAY	JUN
7	16.6	13.3	FEB	MAR	APR	MAY	JUN	JUL
8	18.4	14.7	MAR	APR	MAY	JUN	JUL	AUG
9	20.0	16.0	APR	MAY	JUN	JUL	AUG	SEP

Jake found the May column on side one. He went down the column two rows to July and then across to the required percentages. Two months out the Magic Chart required a return of 8.4% if sold and 6.7% if expired. The corresponding returns for WMT were 3.01 and 4.35 at a strike price of 55. For a strike price of 57.50 the returns were 5.29 and 2.15. Jake quickly did the same comparison on the September and December expirations.

"Professor, none of the returns I computed on my Wal-Mart stock meet the requirements of the Magic Chart. I agree with what you said earlier about beating the return on a CD. Any of the options would do that. But, what does it mean that WMT compares so unfavorably with what you look for in option premium."

Rob smiled. "What it means Jake is that my standards are high. On virtually any good stock you can earn a strong return by selling options. But I look for the real gems. There are always good quality stocks on which the option premium will meet the Magic Chart. But they are not just lying around. You don't find diamonds just lying around. It takes effort to find the gems.

"Later, I will show how to search the market. But for now let's be sure you have the basics. Good job on the homework assignment. Now let's get some of the basic terminology for options down."

Rob paused for a sip of tea. It had gotten cool. As if reading his mind Tiffany appeared with a pot of hot water and topped off both cups, leaving also fresh tea bags.

Jake was taking notes. Two competing thoughts were going through his mind: *Why didn't I know about this sooner?* And, *Perhaps I can become a master of selling Covered Calls and Naked Puts! Create my own monthly cash income.*

"I'm ready," he said. "Let's take the next step."

"Good. Let's cover some basic information about options.

"You can trade options on most stocks just as easily as trading the stock itself. The mechanics of buying and selling are basically the same. The trades are executed through your brokerage account. The significant difference is in the option symbol. A stock symbol tells you the name of the company and that's it. Option trades, however, require additional specifications such as expiration month, strike price and whether the option is a Call or Put. This information is communicated through the option symbol.

"Obviously, all stocks have a stock symbol. For example Wal-Mart is WMT. Options, both Calls and Puts, also have symbols. An option symbol has two parts: 1) the root, which identifies the underlying stock, and 2) a two-letter code, which identifies the type of option (Call or Put), the expiration month and the strike price.

"Looking at an option symbol, after a little practice, you will immediately know the underlying stock, the expiration month, strike price and whether it is a Call or Put. It may seem a little strange at first, but, trust me, it will be second nature in no time."

"Gee, Professor, I hope so. I'm feeling really confused right now. Maybe an example will help."

"Sure," smiled Rob. "Let's continue with Wal-Mart. The root part of the option symbol is WMT, the stock symbol. This will be the case with most New York Stock Exchange stocks but not with NASDAQ stocks. For example Microsoft has a stock symbol of MSFT and option root of MSQ.

"But let's stay focused on Wal-Mart. The root of the option symbol is WMT, the stock symbol. To the root we add two more letters. The first of those two additional letters is a code for the expiration month and whether the option is a Call or Put. Here's the table for that first letter.

Expiration Month

	CALLS	PUTS			CALLS	PUTS
January	A	M		July	G	S
February	B	N		August	H	T
March	C	O		September	I	U
April	D	P		October	J	V
May	E	Q		November	K	W
June	F	R		December	L	X

The second letter is code for the strike price. This code is not as precise as the expiration month. You have to use a little common sense. I'll show you what I mean in a moment. Here's the table for strike price.

Strike Price

A	5, 105, 205	N	70, 170, 270
B	10, 110, 210	O	75, 175, 275
C	15, 115, 215	P	80, 180, 280
D	20, 120, 220	Q	85, 185, 285
E	25, 125, 225	R	90, 190, 290
F	30, 130, 230	S	95, 195, 295
G	35, 135, 235	T	100, 200, 300
H	40, 140, 240	U	7.50, 37.50, 67.50
I	45, 145, 245	V	12.50, 42.50, 72.50
J	50, 150, 250	W	17.50, 47.50, 77.50
K	55, 155, 255	X	22.50, 52.50, 82.50
L	60, 160, 260	Y	27.50, 57.50, 87.50
M	65, 165, 265	Z	32.50, 62.50, 92.50

"Let's go back to your home work assignment and your example for Wal-Mart. The first option you selected was Jul 55. That means the expiration is in July and the strike price is $55.00. So tell me what would be the option symbol for that Call option."

Jake had been listening closely and anticipating just this question. He knew the root for the option would be WMT and that there would be two more letters. The first of the two additional letters would identify the month of July and the fact that it was a Call option, not a Put option. He looked at the Expiration Month table and decided that would be a G. So he wrote down WMTG.

Now he needed the second code letter. This final letter would identify that the strike price was $55.00. Looking at the Strike Price table he found that $55, $155 and $255 were all identified by the letter K.

So the final answer was WMTGK. That was the symbol for a Wal-Mart Call option with expiration in July (G) and which had a strike price of $55 (K).

"Very good," said the professor, knowing that positive feedback is always a good teaching tool. "Now write the symbol for the Wal-Mart option in your homework assignment that has the highest return if CA."

"That should be easy," replied Jake, looking back at his homework assignment. "Let's see. First I know the root is WMT. The one with the highest return if CA is the Dec 57.50. Since it is a Call, and the expiration is December, that will be the 12th letter of the alphabet."

Looking again at the Expiration Month table, Jake found the letter L and wrote down WMTL.

"Now I need the letter that identifies and strike price of $57.50."

Looking at the Strike Price table, Jake quickly found the letter Y. He then wrote down WMTLY.

"Yes," said the professor. "I do believe you've got it. You will be surprised how quickly this becomes second nature. You will soon be able to look at an option symbol and immediately know if it is a Call or Put, and the expiration month and strike price. Of course, when looking at a symbol and deciding what the strike price is will require a little common sense since there are three possible strike prices for each letter. WMTLY could possibly have a strike price of $27.50, $57.50 or $87.50. It depends on which of the three is closest to the current market price of the root stock. For Wal-Mart that obviously means the Y stands for $57.50.

"Now I know you are eager to learn about Puts. But, first let's step back and take an overview. Here's a chart that summarizes all possible Calls and Puts."

Rob pulled the following chart out of his folder and slid it across to Jake.

CALLS		
Buy a Call	**Write (sell) a Call**	
You have the right to purchase a stock at a specified price for a certain period of time.	You have an obligation to sell a stock at a specified price for a certain period of time, if the buyer activates the Call.	
Buy a Put	**Write (sell) a Put**	
You have the right to sell a stock at a specified price for a certain period of time.	You have a obligation to buy a stock at a specified price for a certain period of time, if the buyer activates the Put.	
PUTS		

"As you know, Calls and Puts can be bought and sold," Rob began. "That gives four possible transactions. There are many exotic strategies that make use of various combinations of these four basic transactions. I've examined and used most if not all of them. From my experience your best results will come from the right side of the chart. Remember my motto: *You make money by selling not by buying.*

"Now let's consider the Put option.

"Selling a Put option means you incur the same risk as owning the stock on which you sell the Put. Typically you will sell a Put with a strike price less than the current price of the stock. If the stock goes down you are obligated to buy it at the strike price which may be higher than the market price. If the stock goes up or remains about the same during the option period, the Put will expire.

"What the buyer of the Put option gets is the right to sell you that stock at the strike price until the option period expires. Investors buying Puts are buying insurance against the possibility that the stock will take a dive. You on the other hand, the seller of the Put, have done your homework on the stock and are reasonably confident it is staying relatively flat or going up. We'll get into stock selection later.

"Are you with me so far?"

Jake had been listening carefully and taking notes. "Yes, I think so. One thing I like about the Covered Calls is that in a sense it is risk free. Of course owning stock is not risk free. It can always go down and you have a loss. However, that doesn't seem to be the case with Puts."

"That's right," Rob agreed. "At least that's the way I do it. Some people sell Call options naked, that is without owning the stock. There is tremendous risk in that strategy. If the stock shoots up in price you could be forced to pay that high price for the stock and then immediately sell it at the lower strike price to comply with the option you sold. Naked Calls are very risky. There's no limit to how high the stock could go, even if only temporarily, and create for you a tremendous loss. I always sell Covered Calls, never Naked Calls.

"Now with Puts it's a little different. A Covered Put means selling a Put on a stock that you have already sold short at the same strike price. So if you are forced to buy the stock you are just closing your short position. The money you earned by selling the Put is eaten up by the transaction of selling the stock short and then buying it back.

And of course if the stock goes up the Put option expires, but you lose money on the short sell of the stock. The higher the stock goes the more you lose. Covered Puts are not appealing to me. Perhaps I'm just an optimistic bull and like to design a strategy based on the market going up.

"So in the case of Puts, I sell Naked Puts. There is risk of course. But at least the risk is limited in that the stock cannot go below zero. That's not true of the risk associated with a naked Call. The way I look at a Naked Put is this: Either the stock will go up and the option expires or the stock goes down and I get to buy a desired stock at a discount. If the latter happens I analyze the stock again to make sure it is still desirable and then sell a Covered Call."

Jake was taking notes and rubbing the scar on his left arm. His thoughts briefly wandered back to the shark bite he got while surfing off the coast of Australia many years ago. Shaking his head to clear his mind he said, "Professor I think I need a picture."

"OK. Take a look at this transaction. It's one of my typical Naked Puts."

Rob again slid a single sheet of paper across the table.

5

The Naked Put

Look at market fluctuations as your friend rather than your enemy; profit from folly rather than participate in it.

Warren Buffet

CAREER EDUCATION				CECO	CUY	JAN	APR	JUL	OCT	
12-06-04	S	10	DEC	30.00	.25	229.99	229.99			PE
12-20-04	S	10	JAN	30.00	.80	779.98	1009.97			PE
01-06-05	S	10	FEB	30.00	.50	479.98	1489.95			PE
02-09-05	S	10	MAR	35.00	.90	879.97	2369.92			PE
02-14-05	S	10	FEB	35.00	.65	629.97	2999.89			PE
06-06-05	S	10	OCT	25.00	.75	729.96	3729.85			PE
06-13-05	S	10	JUL	30.00	.75	229.98	3959.83			PE
07-11-05	S	10	AUG	30.00	.35	329.98	4289.81			PE
07-15-05	S	10	AUG	35.00	.70	679.97	4969.78			PE
08-22-05	S	10	JAN	30.00	1.30	1279.95	6249.73			PE
11-08-05	S	10	APR	25.00	1.05	1034.95	7284.68			PE
01-09-06	S	10	JUL	25.00	1.10	1084.96	8369.64			PE
02-03-06	S	10	FEB	30.00	.25	232.49	8602.13			PE
02-07-06	S	10	FEB	30.00	.20	184.99	8787.12			PE
09-18-06	S	10	OCT	20.00	.65	634.98	9422.10			PE
11-06-06	S	20	NOV	17.50	.21	404.98	9827.08			PE
11-21-06	S	10	DEC	22.50	.30	287.99	10115.07			PE
12-05-06	S	10	DEC	22.50	.35	334.98	10450.05			PE
12-07-06	S	10	DEC	22.50	.37	354.98	10805.03			PE

After a few moments Graham said, "Sometimes you get lucky and never have the Naked Puts assigned. Here is an example with Career Education (CECO). Career Education Corporation provides post secondary education primarily in the United States.

"Tell me what you see."

Jake had been studying the chart intently for several minutes. "This may be too good to be true. There's got to be a catch here somewhere. What am I missing?"

Graham just smiled, giving his student time to analyze the Naked Put example further.

"Well," Jake continued, "I remember from the Covered Call chart on IDCC that each line represents a transaction. So on December 6, 2004 you sold Puts on 10 contracts, 1000 shares, of CECO. DEC 30 means the strike price is $30 and the option will expire or be exercised on the third Friday in December. If the stock price is below $30 the holder of the option will require you to buy his 1000 shares for $30. If the stock price is above $30 the option will expire, which is apparently what happened. PE must stand for Put expired. In exchange for selling that option you received $.25 per share or $229.99 net of commission. You continued doing that, selling Naked Puts on CECO, and, over a twenty-four month period ending in December 2006, earned $10,805.03. How did I do?"

"Excellent! Later on I will explain how CECO worked its way to the top of my prospect list. I wouldn't have made these transactions on just any stock. But for now let's focus on the Naked Put as part of the money tree concept.

"Again it is very different from the traditional buy and hold strategy. In fact with Naked Puts I may never own the stock. Of course it has to be a stock that I would be willing to own because the Put might be assigned. But again the concept is to take short-term gains on a continuous basis on stocks that I own (Covered Calls) or stocks that I would be willing to own (Naked Puts). Now I pick some more cash off the money tree for my monthly income account and move on. There are always more trees and more fruit.

"Notice in this example that most of the premiums are for very short periods of time to expiration. I got $.25 per share with only eleven days to expiration. Then I got $.80 per share for thirty-two days to expiration. On August 20, 2005 I got $1.30 per share for four months to expiration. Each one of these premiums provides a discount to the purchase of the stock if you are assigned. The farther out you go the larger the discount."

"I see," Jake exclaimed. "*Time is Money*! So, what is the desired premium for a Naked Put?"

"First, let me clarify what I just said about discount. Let's say a stock is currently selling for $21 and I sell a $20 Put on that stock for a premium of $1.00. My discount on that stock is $2.00. That's my security. The stock will have to go down more then $2.00 before I lose money on the transaction. I could be forced to buy the stock if it goes below $20. But since I receive $1 per share, I wouldn't actually lose money unless the stock fell below $19, a $2 (9.5%) decline.

"Now concerning an acceptable Put, my goal on Naked Puts is to get a premium that is 2% to 10% of the stock price for the shortest time frame possible. That premium represents a discount on the price of the stock in the event I am *PUT* (have to buy) the stock."

"Here are the guidelines when considering Naked Put opportunities. The elements that may affect the possible outcome are:

- Time factor—how long to expiration based on the chosen strike month
- The premium to be earned
- The total discount—premium plus difference between stock price and strike price
- The current stock price.

"The premium is dependent on the strike price in relation to the current stock price, the time factor, volatility of the stock and who knows what else. The Put premium, just like Call premium, is determined by the dynamics of the market.

"Keep in mind I always select a strike price lower than the current market price. That way if I am Put the stock I am getting it at a discount from the current price. That discount plus the premium provides my downside security on the transaction. The greater the excess of the current stock price over the strike price the lower the premium and the less the risk. Naturally, the premium and the risk are directly related.

"We want to combine these factors in a formula in a way that provides good opportunities, but also guides us away from doing the wrong thing. With this in mind, use the following to calculate a Put Factor for your prospects.

$$\text{Put Factor} = \frac{6\,(100\,\text{PR})\,(\text{CP-SP})}{(\text{ME})\,(\text{SP})\,(\text{SP})}$$

Where:
    ME = Months to Expiration
    PR = Put Option Premium
    CP = Current Stock Price
    SP = Strike Price

"I have had excellent success with Naked Puts for stocks when this factor is positive and close to one," said the professor.

"Notice that when looking at Put options, the farther you go out in time at a particular strike price the higher the Put option premium and the larger the discount (but also the higher the risk). It is very difficult to predict what can happen as the time element gets longer, so be careful with the strike price at which you are willing to buy the stock.

"Whenever I get Put option quotes with my VISIONS Stock Market Explorer software the Put Factor is provided, along with all the other important stock and option information to help in the selection process.

"I will give you an example of an analysis with my VISIONS Stock Market Explorer software on CECO that shows what I am looking for before I make a Naked Put selection. Notice the next to last column. Here the software analyzes each Put and gives it a Best Fit ranking. The diamonds, <->, represent the best opportunities based on my Put formula."

```
Put Options for CAREER EDUCATION [CECO] On 10/05/07 9:09 PM TAI=Bad Idea        _ □ ×
Print   Throw Away   Export Data   Get Chart
Put Options for CAREER EDUCATION [CECO] On 10/05/07 9:09 PM TAI=Bad Idea
Price 31.04 (+1.15) 52WkHi 36.68 52WkLow 20.71 50DayAvg 28.28 BL 24.7 BR -15.88 Beta 1.59
```

Option Symbol	Strike Date	Strike Price	Put Premium Bid	Option Premium Asked	Open Interest	Put Factor	Percent Discount	Mths Till Exp	Best Fit	Price If Assigned
CUYWD	11/16/07	20.00	0.05	0.15	19	0.58	0.25	1		19.95
CUYWX	11/16/07	22.50	0.15	0.20	5	1.06	0.67	1	**	22.35
CUYWE	11/16/07	25.00	0.30	0.40	295	1.21	1.20	1	**	24.70
CUYWF	11/16/07	30.00	1.35	1.45	395	0.65	4.50	1		28.65
CUYMC	1/18/08	15.00	0.05	0.10	805	0.61	0.33	3		14.95
CUYMD	1/18/08	20.00	0.35	0.45	2,957	1.64	1.75	3	<->	19.65
CUYME	1/18/08	25.00	1.00	1.10	7,997	1.64	4.00	3	<->	24.00
CUYMF	1/18/08	30.00	2.25	2.35	4,257	0.44	7.50	3		27.75
CUYPC	4/18/08	15.00	0.10	0.20	112	0.65	0.67	6		14.90
CUYPW	4/18/08	17.50	0.25	0.35	219	1.01	1.43	6	**	17.25
CUYPD	4/18/08	20.00	0.50	0.60	107	1.26	2.50	6	***	19.50
CUYPX	4/18/08	22.50	0.85	0.95	258	1.31	3.78	6	***	21.65
CUYPE	4/18/08	25.00	1.35	1.45	320	1.19	5.40	6	**	23.65
CUYPF	4/18/08	30.00	2.85	3.00	123	0.30	9.50	6		27.15

Here is my summary of the Put factor for all the CECO trades.

Put Factors for CECO					
Date	Stock Price	Strike Price	Option Premium	Months to Expiration	Put Factor
12/06/04	39.86	30.00	0.25	0.37	4.48
12/20/04	36.98	30.00	0.80	1.07	3.49
01/06/05	40.32	30.00	0.50	1.43	2.40
02/09/05	40.21	35.00	0.90	1.23	1.86
02/14/05	39.60	35.00	0.65	0.13	10.98
06/06/05	35.45	25.00	0.75	4.57	1.65
06/13/05	38.99	30.00	0.75	1.07	4.21
07/11/05	38.79	30.00	0.35	1.30	1.58
07/15/05	40.60	35.00	0.70	1.17	1.65
08/22/05	37.76	30.00	1.30	5.03	1.34
11/08/05	35.12	25.00	1.05	5.47	1.87
01/09/06	32.42	25.00	1.10	6.43	1.22
02/03/06	33.90	30.00	0.25	0.46	1.41
02/07/06	33.82	30.00	0.20	0.33	1.54
09/18/06	20.48	20.00	0.65	1.10	0.43
11/06/06	21.55	17.50	0.21	0.40	4.17
11/21/06	25.92	22.50	0.30	0.83	1.47
12/05/06	25.61	22.50	0.35	0.36	3.58
12/07/06	25.85	22.50	0.37	0.30	4.90

"Be very cautious if the Put factor is less than one. If it is negative you have selected a strike price that is greater than the current stock price. Make sure this is what you want to do since your chances of assignment are much greater, but still at a discount if the premium is high enough."

Graham paused for a sip of tea and to be sure Jake was following his presentation.

"Jake, you mentioned there must be a catch. Well, there is an investment needed to accomplish a Naked Put trade even though it is not shown on the chart. Since these are Naked Puts, you need sufficient cash or margin in your brokerage account to make these trades. The amount varies by brokerage firm. My broker requires a cash or margin reserve of 20% of the Put purchase price plus the premiums received. If this is a cash reserve, it is earning interest at the broker margin rate, so in a sense one could be double dipping—earning premiums and interest!

"One of my most successful strategies has been what I Call *The Double Up*. Let's say you like a certain stock and would like to invest in it over time, perhaps 2,000 shares. But you are a little concerned about current trend and momentum. That stock is a prime candidate for the *Double Up*. I buy 50% of the desired investment, 1,000 shares in this case, now and sell a Covered Call with strike price reasonably close to the market price. I also sell an equal number of Naked Puts at a strike price lower than the current market price. At this point there will be three possible results:

"**Stock Price Down,** in which case the Puts are assigned (stock is purchased at put strike price), the Calls will expire and I now have my intended investment of 2,000 shares and continue to sell Covered Calls.

"**Stock Price Close to Unchanged,** in which case the Puts and Calls both expire. This is where I started, except I have pocketed nice premiums for selling the Puts and Calls. And I'm ready to repeat the process again, selling Covered Calls and Naked Puts, picking more monthly income off the money tree.

"**Stock Price Up,** in which case the Calls are assigned (stock is sold to the call owner) and the Puts expire. In this case I am

40

back to a total cash position with respect to this investment with a significant gain. At this point I would go back to my prospect list and consider new candidates for another *Double Up* or one of my other strategies.

"Here's an example that illustrates my *Double Up* strategy. The company is SanDisk (SNDK), one of the leading providers of memory cards that are used in portable devices like your digital camera and Blackberry. They just reported record earnings when I started this sequence."

Graham slid the SanDisk chart across the table.

SANDISK CORP					SNDK	SWO	JAN	APR	JUL	OCT
01-10-05	B		1000		24.13	24135.00	-24135.00		
01-10-05	S	10	FEB	22.50	2.75	2729.95	-21405.05	CA
01-10-05	S	10	FEB	20.00	.40	379.98	-21025.07	PE
02-18-05	C		1000		22.50	22480.25	1455.18	<

"I decided that an investment of 2000 shares would be in order. So using my *Double Up* strategy on January 10 I bought 1000 shares at $24.13 and sold February Calls with a $22.50 strike price. I earned $2,729.95 on the transaction. These are called In-The-Money (ITM) Calls since the strike price is smaller then the current stock price. The stock market was in a downward trend in early January 2005. I picked a strike price below market to provide myself with some downside protection. In other words SNDK could go down to $21.38 from where I bought it before I would lose money on this investment. For the second stage of the *Double Up* strategy I sold 10 contracts of February Puts with a strike price of $20."

My cautious approach was effective. Of the three possible results I mentioned earlier the result was **Stock Price Up**. The 1000 shares on which I had sold Calls were assigned (purchased) for $22.50 and the Put contracts I had sold expired.

"I earned $1,455.18 in 39 days. I had $22,480.25 invested for a gain of 6.47%. Not bad for just 39 days.

"So, are you ready to see a few more examples of *Double Up*?"

"Sock it to me," Jake exclaimed with a big grin.

"Here are two more interesting companies," Graham said as he looked through his folder. "They demonstrate how you can improve the return on a Covered Call strategy by selling a Naked Put also. The first is Goldcorp, Inc. This company engages in the acquisition, exploration, development, and operation of precious metal properties in the Americas and Australia. Here I did an At-The-Money (ATM) Call and a Naked Put.

"Jake, I see you are getting pretty adept at reading my charts now. What do you see here?"

GOLD CORP					GG	GG	JAN	APR	JUL	OCT
03-27-07	B		1000	24.98			24984.50	-24984.50		
03-27-07	S	10	APR	25.00	.90		884.98	-24099.52		CA
03-27-07	S	10	APR	22.50	.45		434.99	-23664.53		PE
04-20-07	C		1000	25.00			24979.62	1315.09		<

Jake answered, "I see on this chart that you bought 1000 shares, sold a Covered Call at a strike price of $25.00 with April expiration. On the same day you sold a Naked Put at a $22.50 strike price, also April expiration. The stock price was above $25.00 at expiration in April 2007, because the Call was assigned and you ended with all cash. A nifty profit of $1,315.09 or 5.26% in less then one month."

"Right, and it's interesting to me if you break down the profit into two parts," Rob replied. "If I had done only Covered Calls the profit would have been $884.98 or 3.45%. Decent enough, but the Puts boosted the profit by $434.99 adding almost 2% to my gain."

"Here is another *Double Up* investment in Advanced Micro Devices, Inc., a semiconductor company. It provides processing solutions for the computing, graphics, and consumer electronics markets in the United States, Europe, and Asia. It offers single-core and dual-core microprocessor products for servers, workstations, notebooks, and desktop personal computers."

ADVANCED MICRO DEVICES				AMD	AMD JAN	APR JUL	OCT	
08-08-07	B		2000	13.03		26065.00	-26065.00	
08-08-07	S	20	SEP	13.00	.88	1739.97	-24325.03	CA
08-08-07	S	20	SEP	11.00	.49	959.98	-23365.05	PE
09-21-07	C		2000	13.00		25979.61	2614.56	<

"Again my monthly income was enhanced by adding Puts to the basic Covered Call strategy with an overall gain of 10.06% in less then two months.

"There is one more variation that I use. Before I get to that Jake, would you like to summarize for me what we've covered so far. Just want to make sure I'm not going too fast for you."

"Sure," Jake looked quickly at his notes. "We started off with . . . I guess you would Call it a pure Naked Put. With Career Education you sold numerous Puts and they all expired. How would you compute your return on that?"

Graham smiled, shrugged his shoulders and said, "Perhaps with the potential investment of an assigned Put. But you might notice on all my investments, my primary goal is to return to a cash position. After a while you get a feel for how much cash you should be acquiring with my Covered Calls and Naked Puts strategy."

Jake looked over his notes again and continued. "So the first one is the pure Naked Put where all your Puts expire and you never actually own the stock. And the second one is the *Double Up* where you buy half of your intended investment and sell Puts for the other half. And you say there is one more. Is it a case where you intend to have a pure Naked Put but you have to buy the stock?"

"Jake, that's good thinking. The dream of every teacher is to impart their own knowledge into the hungry minds of their students."

Staying on track, Graham went on, "Always, when I sell a Put, it is on a stock that I would not mind buying, especially at the discounted strike price. So I know that's a possibility.

"If you are assigned (put) a stock at expiration, you can always sell it the next trading day if you feel things have changed and you don't want to own the company.

"This is exactly what I did with an assignment of General Motors (GM) stock on December 16, 2005," said the professor.

"Here is the data on GM:

GENERAL MOTORS					GM	GM JAN	APR	JUL	OCT
03-23-05	S	40	SEP	15.00	.55	2134.92	2134.92		PE
03-29-05	S	10	MAY	25.00	.65	629.97	2764.89		PE
05-26-05	S	10	JUL	27.50	.40	379.98	3144.87		PE
06-06-05	S	10	JUN	30.00	.55	529.97	3674.84		PE
11-18-05	S	30	JUN	10.00	1.10	3272.36	6947.20		PE
11-21-05	S	10	DEC	22.50	.80	784.96	7732.16		PA
11-21-05	S	20	DEC	17.50	.12	219.98	7952.14		PE
12-06-05	S	40	MAR	7.50	.40	1564.92	9517.06		PE
12-16-05	B		1000		22.50	22519.00	-13001.94		
12-19-05	S		1000		22.16	22154.91	9152.97		<

"In early 2005, GM came out with guidance that indicated they were going to have negative earnings. On the first big drop in the stock I waited a few weeks and after the price stabilized at about 28 I felt a September 15 Put was safe. I received $.55 per share and was willing to buy 4000 shares at $15.00 and had the account margin to cover it.

"GM did recover somewhat after Kerkor "Kirk" Kerkorian made a huge investment at $31.00 a share. The September $15.00 Puts therefore expired worthless. The person who gambled on buying the Puts was again out the premium.

"Then the stock went down again to a low of $21.19 on November 16, 2005. I saw the opportunity to sell additional Puts.

"The stock was down in late December and I was Put 1000 shares at $22.50 on Friday, December 16. The current news surrounding GM at the time was not so good, so to be safe I immediately sold the 1,000 shares on the following Monday at $22.16 and still came out with a small gain of $420.87 (22154.91 + 784.96—22519.00) on the transaction.

"When you follow this strategy you must be ready to buy a stock when a Put is assigned, but you can also take action (sell in this case) to reduce potential risk.

"How about another one? Here is a twelve month stock price chart of PLXS (Plexus Corp.). Plexus, together with its subsidiaries, operates in the electronics manufacturing services industry."

"Notice how the stock price moves up and down during the twelve month period. It started at $25 in August 2006, then went down to about $19 and then up to $27 in November 2006. It then started down again and hit a low of $16 in March 2007. After this low it started a new up trend for the next five months."

"This type of stock price cycle provides a great opportunity for significant gains with Covered Calls and Naked Puts.

"Here is the trade data for the first up cycle in November 2006.

PLEXUS CORP				PLXS	QUA	MAR JUN SEP DEC		
11-01-06	B		800	22.00		17604.50	-17604.50	
11-01-06	S	8	NOV	22.50	1.05	829.47	-16775.03	CA
11-01-06	S	10	NOV	20.00	.55	537.98	-16237.05	PE
11-17-06	C		800	22.50		17991.89	1754.84	<
						GAIN/LOSS	9.96	%

"I did an Out-Of-The-Money call at a strike price of $22.50 and a naked put at a strike price of $20. The stock made a move up and I was called out. This set of trades had a 9.96% gain in sixteen days.

"The stock was now above its buy limit, so I kept it on my prospect list for future action."

"After about six months it again traded below its buy limit and then started an up trend such that it became a good investment candidate in May 2007."

PLEXUS CORP						PLXS	QUA MAR JUN SEP DEC		
05-23-07	B		1200	22.52			27028.46	-27028.46	
05-23-07	S	12	JUL	22.50	1.30		1546.48	-25481.98	CA
05-23-07	S	10	JUL	20.00	.35		337.99	-25143.99	PE
07-20-07	C		1200	22.50			26991.92	1847.93	<
							GAIN/LOSS	6.84	%

"This time I did an At-The-Money call at a strike price of $22.50 and another naked put at $20. The stock again moved up and I was called out for a gain of 6.84% in two months.

"Look at the stock price at the end of this chart. It is almost the same as it was twelve months earlier. If all one did is buy and hold, your gain would be nothing. By riding the wave with Covered Calls and Naked Puts I generated a significant gain and monthly income on my holdings."

"One could also sell only Naked Puts against an all cash account. The strategy is that you would only begin to own any stocks through the assignment of a Put. All of your stock purchases are then at a discount. Again you would only do this with companies you would like to own but at a lower price."

Rob paused to reflect on what they had covered so far. "You know Jake, getting back into teaching after all these years is a new experience. I'm concerned that I might leave something out that's really important. The Plexus example reminds me of an important concept we should cover with relation to which option you sell, whether call or put. I call it riding the wave."

6

Riding the Wave

Always bear in mind that your own resolution to
succeed is more important than any other.

Abraham Lincoln

"Remember this Jake. Stock prices do not always continue to go up. They cycle through various price points, making a new 52-week high and then a new 52-week low. If you watch the stock prices of good companies, over time you will be able to detect the pattern that will allow you to buy at the right time and sell Calls and Puts that provide a steady monthly income stream. I call this process riding the wave."

"Fundamental to riding the wave, both up and down, is a clear understanding of the market trend on the type of option you sell. By that I mean whether the option is In the Money (ITM), At the Money (ATM) or Out of the Money (OTM).

"Let me summarize for you just when to use these different strategies, depending on the individual stock and overall market trend.

"**Sell In-The-Money (ITM) Covered Calls** if there is concern that the stock may go down. ITM means the strike price is below the market price. The premium you receive has both an intrinsic value (that difference between strike price and market price) and time value (the gamble by the purchaser of the Call that the stock will shoot up). The more one is in-the-money the greater the downside protection one has, but at the cost of a lower gain. Remember Insurance does cost money. This is a good strategy for short-term gains that beat money market or CD rates.

"**Sell At-The-Money (ATM) Covered Calls** if it appears that the stock (or market) is flat and going nowhere. ATM means the strike price and market price are very close to the same. Any difference between the two is negligible. The downside protection is only the premium received. The gain can be excellent if done over and over.

"**Sell Out-of-The-Money (OTM) Covered Calls** when a stock is in a good up trend and the overall market is rising (a rising tide lifts all boats). OTM means the strike price is higher than the current market price. The gain is not only the premium received (which provides some downside protection) but also potentially from stock appreciation. The stock appreciation is received only if the stock is called. If a stock does not go up far enough to be called you get the "If Expired" gain. Gain from appreciation is not experienced until you sell at a higher price. The gain here can be significant.

"**Sell Out-of-The-Money (OTM) Naked Puts** on good stocks at a strike price below the market price. This may be a bit confusing. You have to understand that an OTM Put has a strike price below the market price and an OTM Call has a strike price above the market price. The key attribute they have in common is zero intrinsic value, only time value. Keep in mind that a Put increases in value as a stock goes down. A Call increases in value as the stock goes up. An OTM Call is when the strike price is above the current market price. An OTM Put is just the opposite. An OTM Put is when the strike price is below market price. That makes sense because your objective with a Put is to buy the stock at a discount if the Put is assigned. For that to happen the strike price (price at which you may be assigned the stock) must be below the current market price when you sell the Put.

"In summary, I routinely do ATM, ITM and OTM Calls, but I only do OTM Puts.

"For Puts you need cash or margin in your account to cover a possible assignment. Do this on stocks that you are considering for Covered Calls. Buy half now, sell a Covered Call and also sell an equal number of Naked Puts at a strike price below the market price (*Double Up* strategy). This concept can enhance the gain by a number of percentage points over a straight Covered Call."

Rob paused and looked at Jake , wondering if perhaps he was going too fast.

Jake understood and responded, "I will need to go over my notes and make sure I understand all this. But I do have one question now. Any guidelines on what percentage of your trades are in Puts?"

"Limit yourself to 20% or less of the account value that you have tied up supporting Naked Puts. One way to look at Puts is as a vehicle to preplan some of your new investments. My main focus is Covered Calls. But because some of the Calls will be assigned resulting in extra cash, you might as well be buying good stocks at a discount."

"OK, that makes sense," Jake replied. He noticed he was unconsciously rubbing the scar on his left arm. Remembering the shark attack was a sign that he was troubled about an important pending decision. A moment's thought brought it to the surface.

"Uh, professor, one more question. I'm eager to get started generating a monthly cash income by selling options. Katie and I have a portfolio of about 15 stocks. But this is all so new. I mean what do I do first? At the last Rotary meeting you took a random selection of stocks from the members and used that program, I recall PIE but what did it stand for?"

"PIE stands for Portfolio Income Explorer. It's part of my VISIONS package that I use to find and analyze stocks and options.

Rob continued, "Yes, PIE is certainly an attention getter. People are always amazed at the amount of income that can be released from an average portfolio—or the Dow 30 for that matter.

"I understand your question. You want to apply PIE to your own portfolio, find out how much money you're leaving on the table so to speak. And you are probably also wondering about the quality of your selection of stocks. Am I right?"

"Yes! Exactly. We've covered Calls and Puts. My head is throbbing.

But I'm beginning to realize this is a much bigger subject. How do I know if I've got good stocks?"

"Excellent!" exclaimed Rob. "You have asked the really key question. I've seen get-rich-quick schemes based on stock options. They all omit or gloss over the really key question which is how to select good stocks in the first place."

Rob glanced at the time on his PDA. "Not enough time today. We'll save it for next session, after Rotary next week."

Jake quickly grabbed the restaurant bill. "My treat. I wonder if Tiffany would rather have a cash tip or a stock tip," he said with a smile.

As the two men walked out to the parking lot the professor had one final question.

"Jake are you familiar with the two basic approaches to stock analysis?

"Hmmm. I think I know, but refresh my memory.

"They are known as Fundamental Analysis and Technical Analysis. My plan begins with the fundamentals to be sure I have solid companies. Then I use the technicals to time the transactions. They are both important."

The door of the Bentley swung open in a warm greeting with the triumphant sounds of Beethoven's *Eroica* emanating from the stereo system. "See you next Thursday. We've got a lot to cover."

7

Build the Prospect List

Create your own vision of happiness.
Jean Groenke

The Rotary Club meeting ended and Jake waited patiently as Rob met the Membership Chairman and filled out the paperwork to be proposed for membership. Tiffany greeted them with a bright smile and led them to a secluded table.

"We have some special herbal tea I would like for you to try. I'll be right back." And off she bustled.

Rob noticed how diligently Jake was going over his notes as they settled into their seats. "I seem to recall that you made an A in my Finance 101 course."

Jake laughed. "No not exactly professor. I had an A going into the final. But then I got distracted toward the end of the semester. Her name is Katie. I would like for you to meet her. We've been blessed with three daughters and five spectacular grandkids."

"That's wonderful. Jean and I enjoy our kids and grandkids too. But let's get back to business. I've got two questions for you. First, do you understand the money tree concept?"

"I think so," Jake responded as he gathered his thoughts. "To me it's a rather radical concept for investing. Different from all my traditional understanding. We had a speaker at the Forum Club in Naples recently. A guy named John Bogle. He made a lot of sense. His strategy seems to be to invest in an index fund, keep transaction costs low and ride the market up over the long term. Last week Katie and I had Tiffany and her boy friend over for lunch. Nice guy I guess, but really not good enough for Tiff. Anyway, she was telling about the investing philosophy of her investment club. If I remember correctly . . ."

"I heard that!" Tiffany had good ears and was just coming around the corner with their herbal tea.

Winking at Rob, "He's never liked any of my boy friends. Cut me some slack Uncle Jake. A girl's got to have a little fun."

Jake began to blush and Rob commented, "Tiffany, Jake was telling me about the philosophy of your investment club. Could you explain it?"

"Sure. Our local investment club is a member of NAIC. They provide a lot of support, monthly magazine and such. There are four basic principles. Make regular investments, reinvest all earnings and dividends, invest in growth equities, and diversify. But like I said earlier, the concept of options has never come up. Why do you think that is?"

"My guess," Rob responded "is they are not familiar with how conservative and risk free a Covered Call transaction is. Like most people when they think of options trading they are thinking of buying rather than selling. But actually my strategy would be perfect for an investment club. I've worked out a rational process of stock selection and ranking. And, having done it both ways, I much prefer the money tree concept. By the way Jake was just explaining his understanding of the concept. Can you join us?"

"No, I've got to get back to the front. But how about giving a presentation to our investment club?"

"Be glad to. Set it up and let me know." As she left, "Okay Jake, tell me about the money tree concept. That's my first of two questions for you."

"Obviously it's entirely different from the traditional investing that you hear from John Bogle or learn in investment clubs. The key there is stock appreciation over time. With the money tree concept you are more interested in how much fruit you can pick off the tree rather than how tall the tree may grow. In the case of Calls you are happy if your stock gets bought. And in the case of Puts you may never even own the stock. I see definite advantages. You have short-term relationships with stocks so you are not likely to get emotionally involved. And you get paid up front when you sell a Call or Put. That money is yours no matter what. Oh, and one other thing. You make money even in a stagnant market. And perhaps even in a down market like that investment you showed me in COTT. You don't need stock appreciation to make money. That's about it. How did I do?"

"Very good. I think you've got it. Now here's your second question. What does the money tree concept have in common with the investment club philosophy?"

Jake was surprised at the question. He finally understood how different the two concepts were. How could they have any thing in common?

"Gee professor, I'm drawing a blank. They seem to be entirely opposite." Glancing over his notes he suddenly had a thought.

"Oh, maybe I've got it. Could it be what you said we would cover next after the money tree concept? Building a qualified prospect list and ranking the stocks. I understand that's also the main topic of discussion in investment club meetings, the merits of various stock candidates for investing. Am I right?"

"Absolutely. The most important decision before selling a Call or Put is stock selection." Rob glanced at the time feature on his PDA. "I'm meeting Jean in 30 minutes. Let's talk about building a qualified prospect list and then we will cover ranking the stocks later.

"Remember, at this point we are simply building a qualified prospect list and organizing it into marketplace or technology areas with three or four companies in each area. We are like the owner of a major league baseball team. We want a lot of players on the farm team. And of course we want to develop player-prospects for each position. But just because a stock makes it onto the prospect list does not mean we are about to buy it. Many farm league players never make it to the big league. Using my software program we easily sort the list to determine our best prospects. My prospect list includes stocks I've bought and those on which I've sold a Naked Put. I continue to include them in the ranking process to be sure they are still viable.

"There is no limit to how many stocks you can have on your prospect list. But each stock you include must pass the following seven tests."

With that Rob slid a sheet of paper across the table to Jake with the following criteria:

1) An options market must exist for the stock.
2) Annual sales or revenue of at least $250 million per year ($500 million is desirable).
3) Market Cap of $500 million or more ($750 million is desirable).
4) Positive revenue growth (10–15% per year is desirable).
5) Positive earnings for three of the last four quarters (positive for the last four quarters is desirable).
6) Average daily trading volume of at least 250,000 shares per day (500,000 shares per day is desirable).
7) Positive Bare Cash ($100 million or more is desirable). Bare Cash is cash plus marketable securities less long term debt.

"Any Questions on these criteria?" Rob asked.

Jake carefully looked over the list. As he went down the list he was nodding his head in agreements. Until . . .

"Positive Bare Cash? Professor this number seven, I don't think I've ever heard of it. Cash plus marketable securities less long-term debt. I can see the obvious value of the first six. But what's the significance of #7?

"Bare Cash was the last addition to my list of selection criteria. After analyzing my successful trades I discovered that the underlying companies that were very profitable in many cases had lots of cash and very little long-term debt on their balance sheet. Now some analysts believe that long-term debt is okay because it gives the company leverage. That sounds right, but debt is not free. It is carried at some interest rate and must be serviced. Monies to service the debt must come from somewhere and usually come out of earnings.

"When I find a company with positive Bare Cash I know a couple of things which are very comforting. First, I know that the burden of servicing debt is not going to be a drag on cash flow. And second, I know that liquid assets are on hand to meet contingencies that are bound to occur.

"When the economic cycle bottoms, those companies with lots of positive Bare Cash are able to grow and in many cases gain market share from the competition. During these times you see many lay-offs and downsizings. Check out the balance sheet of the companies involved and you will see for yourself.

"Positive Bare Cash gives a company staying power and a competitive advantage. These are the ones we want on our prospect list."

Jake gave a final nod of his head. "Yes, I agree. That's the way I arrange my personal finances. No debt and no interest payments."

"Very good," agreed Rob. "Now let me make a few more comments about your prospect list.

"By the way these seven criteria represent the Fundamental Analysis aspect that I mentioned last week. It's important to build your prospect list with solid companies.

Now, you have to search for good companies since they are not obvious. You should first look in an industry or market that you are familiar with. No matter what your background is, you probably can name thirty to fifty companies very quickly that touched your life in the last twenty-four hours one way or another. From the cereal you had for breakfast, the type of vehicle you drive, the brand of gas you use, the last store you shopped, to the computer on your desk, there are various companies that could have filled your needs. You picked certain ones because of a fuzzy feeling for the product or good advertising on the company's part. I like the computer and communications networking business. I therefore have a prospect list that is weighted heavily in the computer systems, software, networking, and semiconductor markets. I have supplemented this list with companies in the retail, defense, financial services, medical technology, and air transportation areas.

"Identify several marketplace or technology areas that you like and understand. There are a number of places to find these candidates. You could research the Dow 30 members, look at all 500 stocks in the S&P 500, or search the entire market."

"I always consider stocks that are in the highest volume of shares traded for the day as prospects. High volume is important for two reasons. First, you want to always have a market for your stocks. High volume indicates high liquidity. Second, high volume indicates that the market has scrutinized the company very closely. When the market focuses intently on a company, all information available is reflected in the price of the stock. You can then conclude that the stock is accurately priced by the market. No hidden surprises are likely. Look also at the percent gainers and losers list for the day. Check the news. Why did a particular stock go up or down so much in one day? Maybe an analyst upgraded or downgraded the stock, the company beat or missed their earnings estimate, there is new competition, there is a take over rumor or the rumor has been dispelled, etc. There are many reasons. Something major happened and in many cases it is temporary so this may be an opportunity worth tracking.

"I also have found many prospects by looking at the major markets daily and weekly new low lists. Every company has a 52-week high and low. Stocks do go up and down. When good companies hit a new low this is the time to place them on your prospect list and start tracking them. At some point they will move up from this new low and that may be the time we want to get in. We want to buy low and sell Calls as the stock moves up. All of this information is available in the Wall Street Journal and Investors Business Daily or on various web sites like Yahoo Finance and Market Watch."

Rob pulled a sheet of paper out of his notebook and handed it to Jake. "Here's a list of thirty six stocks on my prospect list which I have arranged in 12 groups of three. This is just an example. Actually I have over 100 stocks that I track as prospects. You will need to form your own list based on your particular interests and field of expertise."

ROB GRAHAM PROSPECT LIST	
WalMart (WMT)	Oracle (ORCL)
Costco (COST)	Microsoft(MSFT)
Target (TGT)	Symantec (SYMC)
Imclone (IMCL)	Sandisk (SNDK)
Pfizer (PFE)	Seagate Technology (STX)
Merck (MRK)	Western Digital (WDC)
Agilent Tech (A)	Cisco Systems (CSCO)
Cree Inc (CREE)	Juniper Networks (JNPR)
Citrix Systems (CTXS)	Brocade Communications (BRCD)
Lockheed Martin (LMT)	Sun Micro (JAVA)
General Dynamics (GD)	Hewlett Packard (HPQ)
Honeywell (HON)	Dell Computers (DELL)
JetBlue Airways JBLU)	Cardinal Health (CAH)
Southwest Airlines (LUV)	Boston Scientific (BSX)
AirTran (AAI)	Medtronic (MDT)
Best Buy (BBY)	Bank of America (BAC)
Circuit City (CC)	Goldman Sacks (GS)
Radio Shack (RSH)	Morgan Stanley (MS)

Jake had written down the seven tests for stocks to pass before being included on his prospect list. "Professor, concerning the data for the tests, how do I get that information?"

"No problem. I can . . ."

Just then Rob's PDA gave a soft buzz just as Tiffany rounded the corner with an excited expression. "Yes Jean, I'm leaving in two minutes. Love you."

"Professor," Tiffany exclaimed. "I just talked to the president of our investment club. We had a cancellation and our planned guest speaker cannot come tonight. Could you fill in?"

8

Buy Low—Sell High

The people who are buying stocks because they're going up and they don't know what they do deserve to lose money.

Jim Cramer

The investment club met at the home of its president, Nicholas Gardner, a past president of the Chamber of Commerce and a leading citizen on Marco Island.

Tiffany introduced Professor Graham and Jake to Nicholas and wife, Kris. Members mingled and nibbled on cheese and crackers. The Gardner home was at the end of a street, typical of Marco Island, with a wide canal on each side and bay to the front. The house was surrounded on three sides with water to take full advantage of the spectacular view.

Jake and Tiffany took seats as Nicholas called the meeting to order. "Tonight, we are pleased to have a retired finance professor and new resident of Marco Island as our speaker. Please give your attention to Dr. Rob Graham."

There was friendly applause as Rob stood beside the flip chart facing the group of investors.

"Thank you Nicholas, and members, and especially Tiffany for inviting me tonight. It's always a pleasure to share investment information with interested, intelligent investors. I'm somewhat familiar with

59

NAIC. I admire your dedication to periodic investing and your diligent analysis of individual stocks. As you know, there are many very complicated and sophisticated methods of stock analysis. Over the course of my teaching career I've explored the intricacies of fundamental analysis and technical analysis. Each has its pros and cons. But in the final analysis, what it all comes down to is the old cliché: Buy Low—Sell High."

Graham flipped the chart open. "When you look at the history of each stock in your portfolio you see that each stock was purchased at some point in a cycle of highs and lows which has now become evident. At the time of purchase you don't really know if the cycle is continuing as before or has just turned. We can look back and see that some were bought at a low point in the cycle and then moved up. Some were bought at a high point in the cycle and then moved down. Those in the later group may have now moved back up. Over time, your gain is greatest in those stocks, which you bought at the low point of their cycles.

"A question I asked myself is: 'Is there anyway to increase the odds that I am buying at the low point of the cycle?' Take the two extremes. At the end of each trading day there are stocks, which have closed at a 52-week high. And there are also stocks that closed at a 52-week low. Assuming you have eliminated consideration of stocks with low liquidity, negative earnings or declining sales—just looking at those two groups, the new 52-week highs and the new 52-week lows— which stocks are most likely to be at the bottom of their cycle?

"I offer no guaranties, but I have personally been very successful with stocks moving up from their 52 week low.

"The formulas I will give you now are to compute what I call Buy Limit and Buy Rank. These two values allow me to very quickly filter my prospect list and rank the stocks. For every stock you can get its lowest price of the past 52 weeks and its highest price. Let L stand for the 52 week low and H stand for the 52 week high. The Buy Limit formula is as follows." Rob wrote the following formula on the flip chart.

$$\text{Buy Limit} = L + .25 \times (H - L)$$

"Ideally we would like to buy at L, the 52 week low. But we accept the fact that we cannot time the market and know that an even lower L tomorrow will not supersede today's L. But it is possible we can catch the stock on the way up from L and that's our objective here. The critical increment is .25 (H—L). For example if a stock has a 52-week low of $10 and a 52-week high of $40 then the critical increment is $7.50. That's computed by taking 25% of $40 minus $10. You might think of 7.50 as our window of opportunity. I would be interested in buying the stock in the price range from $10 to $17.50. As we get closer to $17.50, the *Buy Limit*, I begin losing interest in the stock. At $17.50 it is too high. It's easy to see the trend when you are looking at a historical chart of the stock's prices.

"Now we use the Buy Limit in the following formula to compute the Buy Rank for each stock. Let's let BL stand for Buy Limit and CP stand for the Current Price of the stock. Here is the formula for computing the Buy Rank. Notice that the denominator is the critical increment we computed to use in the last formula.

$$\text{Buy Rank} = \frac{10 \times (BL - CP)}{.25 \times (H - L)}$$

"When the current stock price is the same as the 52-week low the buy rank is 10. This is its maximum value. When the current stock price is the same as the 52-week high, the buy rank is negative 30. Our Buy Rank formula gives us a range of values on a scale from negative 30 to positive 10."

Rob drew the following on the flip chart below the two formulas.

-30   0   +5   ↓   +10

"A stock captures my attention with a Buy Rank between 10 and 5, moving down. A decreasing value in the Buy Rank indicates the stock is moving up in price and perhaps has started its next major up trend.

"For example, using our example of a stock with 52-week low of $10 and 52 week high of $40, we computed the Buy Limit to be $17.50. Suppose the current price were $12. At that price we are well below our Buy Limit of $17.50. What is the Buy Rank? First, compute the numerator or top of the fraction: 10(17.50—12) = 55. The denominator is still 7.50, which we computed earlier as .25(H-L). Dividing the numerator, 55, by the denominator, 7.50, we get a Buy Rank of 7.33.

As the current price rises closer to the Buy Limit the Buy Rank declines, approaching zero. For example, a current price of $16 gives a Buy Rank of two. A current price of $17 gives a Buy Rank of 0.66. And of course a current price of $17.50, the same as the Buy Limit, would give a Buy Rank of zero. So we are only interested in stocks with a positive Buy Rank.

"Are there any questions?"

Nicholas stood up, rubbing his chin and still looking at the simple formulas. "Professor Graham, this reminds me of Tiger Woods playing golf. He makes it look easy," said Nicholas. "With mastery comes ease of application and explanation. Did you originate these formulas?"

"I can honestly say I haven't seen them anywhere else," replied Graham. "When I started building my prospect list I began intuitively looking at the list each day of stocks trading at their 52-week low. Frequently the stock would be down because of a bit of sensational news and the market had over reacted. If the fundamentals were good I would add that stock to my prospect list. Also, it seemed obvious to me that the greatest potential losses would come from stocks trading at 52-week highs."

A murmur went through the group as various members mentioned stocks the club bought that had resulted in losses.

"Don't feel alone. We've all made investments that logically should have been great but, nevertheless, turned sour."

With a rueful smile Nicholas commented, "Our group got excited about Symantec last fall. We had lots of discussions and analysis. Wall Street analysts had a buy recommendation on the stock. Finally, in October of 2006, we bought in at about $21 a share. It has not gone anywhere since."

"That's interesting," Graham replied. "Symantec is a stock that I've had success with. I followed my Buy Limit and Buy Rank rules and did very well. I like the company. It is a world leader in Internet security technology. It also provides a broad range of content and network security solutions to individuals and enterprises. Take a look at my investment strategy with Symantec."

All the members were interested in finding a way they could avoid their recent debacle. Graham noticed a large high definition TV screen behind the flip chart. "Nicholas, do you mind if I use your TV screen? I can show you my investment in Symantec."

Nicholas quickly turned the TV on and removed the flip chart. Graham punched commands into his PDA.

"Symantec (SYMC) has been on my prospect list since 2003. To do our analysis, we need some pertinent information about the stock. I might have mentioned earlier that the Internet provides this information for free. One favorite of mine is www.marketwatch.com. Enter a stock symbol and then go to "Profile."

Here's the key information for October 3, 2006 when your club made its investment in SYMC."

The following information was displayed on the TV screen.

SYMC stock price $21.14
52-week high—$24.00
52-week low—$14.89
50-day average stock price—$18.42
Revenue of over $4 billion per year.
Market Cap of over $18 billion.
Sales growth of 19.5% for the year.
Earnings were positive the past three quarters.
Bare Cash of over $2 billion.
Average number of shares traded per day of over fifteen
   million shares.

Graham continued, "The fundamentals pass my seven tests. Everything looks great and I'm not surprised that your club decided to buy. But for me there was one big warning: The stock price exceeded my Buy Limit. Here's the Buy Limit and Buy Rank calculation with my Buy Limit, Buy Rank Wizard.

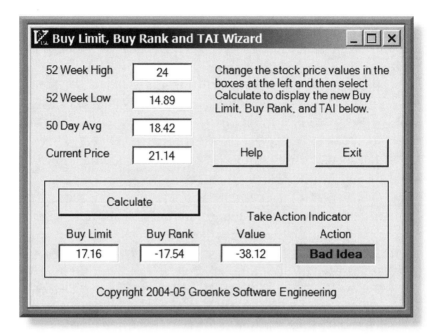

"The Buy Rank is -17.54 which indicates to me that it was a bad idea at that time. At a market price of $21.14 the stock is approaching its 52-week high of $24.00. " That could be a problem if the market goes down or there is a downgrade of the stock, or some negative news.

"Now lets take a look at when I made my move with SYMC. Moving the calendar back to January 30, 2006."

Here is the data:

SYMC stock price $18.19
52-week high—$24.34
52-week low—$16.61
50-day average stock price—$18.01

"Using these values in the Wizard we get a Buy Limit of 18.54 and a Buy Rank of 1.81.

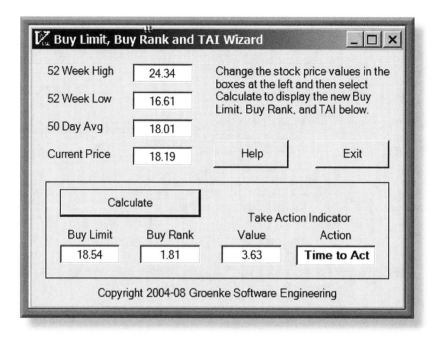

"Everything looks good at this point. Before finally making the investment I also check to see where the stock is trading in relation to its fifty-day moving average. I like to get the very best odds I can," Rob explained. "I've found that it's not enough to have a stock with a good Buy Rank and good return for selling Calls. Those are both critically important. But I want to be as sure as possible that the stock has actually started another up trend. So before investing, I look at a picture of the stock. Here is where a picture could be worth thousands of dollars. I want to see the current price pass through the 50-day moving average. As long as the current price is leading the average down, don't invest. This is what was happening after the big drop in November until the turn up in early January.

"When the price breaks above the 50-day moving average, I feel encouraged that we have begun an up trend. I have noted the different lines on this chart.

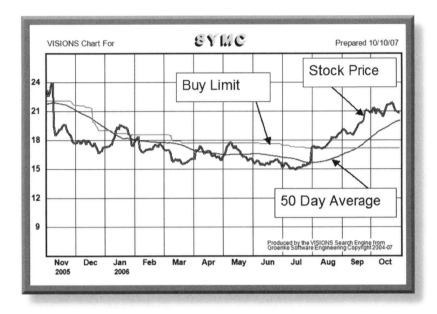

On January 30, 2006 with the stock trading above the 50 day average and at the Buy Limit I did the following." Graham punched on his PDA.

SYMANTEC CORP						SYMC SYQ	JAN	APR JUL OCT
01-30-06	B		1300	18.22		23689.44	-23689.44	
01-30-06	S	13	APR	17.50	1.75	2129.93	-21559.51	CE
04-24-06	S	13	OCT	17.50	1.05	1345.20	-20214.31	CA
10-20-06	C		1300	17.50		22729.31	2515.00 <	

"I bought 1300 shares at $18.22 and sold ITM (In-The-Money) Covered Calls three months out with a $17.50 strike price. The $2,129.93 I received is an 8.99% return for three months on the $23689.44 investment." Graham paused to let this information sink in with the investment club.

Nicholas was probably the first in the group to begin understanding the accounting method. "Professor, that's really a neat way to analyze your investment. In four compact lines you show everything that happened with this investment. Let's see if we understand this. At first you had an investment of $23,689.44, shown as negative cash. You sold an April Call, which expired and then an October Call. Both Calls brought in cash, which decreased your negative cash position. The October Call was assigned which means you sold the 1300 shares for $17.50 each. That cash inflow brought you to a positive cash position for the investment. To me the most important factor in any business is cash flow. No matter what else happens, you have got to have a positive cash flow."

The professor smiled and nodded.

As the group studied the TV screen Tiffany had the next comment. "Professor, would you explain Covered Calls? I'm not sure I understand exactly what happened."

Professor Graham was pleased that the group was ready to think outside the box. He well understood that the biggest hurdle for investors was to grasp the fact that there was more than one way to increase earnings in the market and take the time to investigate. He was more than happy to help.

"A key reason I bought SYMC, in addition to its good fundamentals and Buy Rank, was that it had good Call option premiums. Before buying the 1300 shares I looked at several different options possibilities. I like to sell options with a strike price slightly above the current price if I think the stock may go up, or at a strike price a little lower than the current price if I am not quite so confidant in the stock's bullish prospects. In this case I was concerned that it may not go up a lot and sold a Call at a strike price lower than my purchase price. In doing this I gave myself some downside protection while still generating an excellent return.

"My strategy was correct. SYMC did not go up much more than where I bought it. In fact, in April 2006, my $17.50 Call expired (denoted by CE at the end of 01–30–06 line). I immediately sold an October $17.50 Call to generate additional income from this holding. In October my stock was called (denoted by CA = Call Assigned). This was about the time that the investment club bought in. I was out with a nice gain and the club was in waiting for appreciation."

Graham looked out over the group sitting in the living room and continued. "My investment strategy involves a concept I refer to as the money tree. Rather than being strictly interested in stock appreciation I pick money off the money tree on a continuous basis by selling options."

Graham asked Nicholas if the investment club ever considered selling options?

"No," Nicholas replied. "I'm not sure why not. I was a finance major and options, or derivatives as they were called, were covered in several courses. But somehow I never considered them for my investment strategy. I don't know why. It just wasn't part of the standard model. But I don't see anything scary about what you just showed us with Symantec."

"Right," Rob agreed. "Contrasting my investment in Symantec with the standard 'buy and hold' strategy you can easily see the value of the money tree approach. Here's another picture."

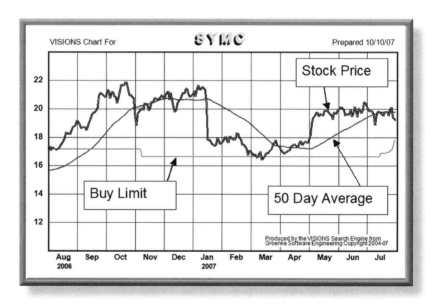

"My stock was called in October 2006. At this point it was trading at $21 and was above the 50-day average, had a Buy Limit of $16.64, and a Buy Rank of -24.92. This Buy Rank indicates that it is a Bad Idea to invest right now."

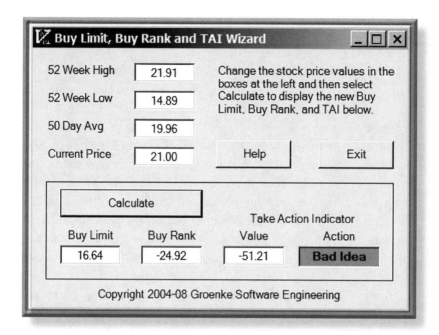

"By imposing the Buy Limit and Buy Rank restraint on myself I avoided buying Symantec at any time other than the low point in its cycle. Symantec had a negative Buy Rank in October of 2006. So I shifted to other stocks in my prospect list, which had a positive Buy Rank.

"This was a good idea, since in January 2007, a number of analysts downgraded the stock and it lost over $3.50 per share. It was down for over three months and then turned up in April 2007. Here is where the investor needs to be ready to do a Covered Call or Naked Put as it moves up through the 50-day average and establishes a new up trend."

One of the club members had pulled his chair up closer to the TV and was intently analyzing the Symantec investment. "Professor, I've got a question."

"Yes sir. Fire away."

"Because you sold those Call options in April 2006, you were forced to sell 1300 shares of Symantec at $17.50. Consequently you missed the run up to $22 in October."

"Yes, that's true," agreed Graham. "But . . . that run up to $22 only benefited investors who sold at that point. That's a day-trader mentality and I do not recommended it.

"Which would you say is more rewarding? Is it better to have the thrill of the ride up and down or is it better to steadily pick money off the money tree by selling options? That's a decision each investor has to decide for him or herself."

There was chatter from the club members as they began discussing the merits of selling options. For most of the members in the investment club it was a brand new concept.

"Professor, you've certainly given us a challenging presentation," said Nicholas. "This is a strategy we all will be discussing at the next meeting. But just one final question so I'm sure I understand. You apparently make money in the stock market by selling options. Does that mean you are not interested in market appreciation?"

Professor Graham searched for the right words to open the minds of the group to what he had to say in conclusion.

"I am interested in market appreciation but not for the same reason as most investors. Your club for example spent a lot of time analyzing various investments and then settled on Symantec at $20. You tried to pick a stock that was going up over the long run. And eventually you may be right. Although you might note that investors who bought RCA at its high point in the 1920s have yet to recover their investment.

"Basically I think you set yourself a very difficult task when you try to pick market winners. The very best stock analysts are seldom right more than 50% of the time. Look at how few mutual funds out perform index funds. And none out perform index funds on a consistent basis.

"But having said that, I am careful about stock selection. I require a positive Buy Rank based on the formulas I showed you. That is a very stringent requirement that has served me well, although certainly not perfect. I've been burned several times with what I thought were good companies. However, any loss that I incurred because the stock went down was cushioned by the premiums I garnered by selling Calls.

"There are basically two reasons I am very careful with stock selection. And these are not the typical reasons you would hear from the

average investor or market analyst. Most investors, like this investment club, are trying to buy the right stocks for price appreciation.
Frankly, as I said, I think that's just too difficult for anyone to do on
a consistent long-term basis. The two reasons I want stocks likely to
go up are:

1) Avoid losses and
2) The option premiums are higher if the market has
   positive expectations for the stock.

"My return on selling options is so good that I don't really need
stock appreciation. What I'm doing is playing good defense as I consistently pick money off the money tree.

"Here is an example of an investment in Whole Foods Market
Inc. (WFMI) in April 2007. Whole Foods Market and its subsidiaries
engage in the ownership and operation of natural and organic foods
supermarkets."

Graham punched WFMI into his PDA and the following information was displayed on the TV screen.

WFMI stock price $47.91
52-week high—$72.53
52-week low—$42.13
50 day average stock price—$45.19
Revenue of over $5 Billion per year.
Market Cap of over $6 billion.
Sales growth of 5.2% for the year.
Earnings were positive the past four quarters.
Bare Cash of over $185 million.
Average number of shares traded per day of over three
million shares.
Buy Limit $49.73
Buy Rank of 2.39

"This appeared to be a good opportunity that meets my criteria and
is starting to move up from a new low at the end of January 2007."

"I reviewed the following chart and decided an investment at this
time was appropriate."

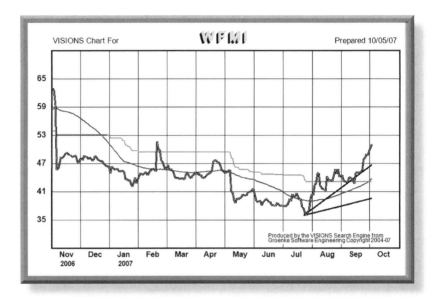

Graham punched on his PDA again and the following trade data was displayed.

WHOLE FOODS MARKET					WFMI	FMQ JAN	APR JUL	OCT
04-27-07	B		500	47.28		23643.25	-23643.25	
04-27-07	S	5	MAY	45.00	3.31	1646.72	-21996.53	CE
05-02-07	B		1000	45.95		45954.71	-67951.24	
05-02-07	S	10	MAY	45.00	2.36	2347.96	-65603.28	CE
05-21-07	S	15	AUG	45.00	.90	1334.23	-64269.05	CE
08-17-07	S	15	SEP	45.00	1.04	1544.23	-62724.82	CE
09-21-07	C		300	45.00		13492.25	-49232.57	CA
09-24-07	S	12	NOV	45.00	2.74	3274.44	-45958.13	CA
11-16-07	C		1200	45.00		53980.10	8021.97	<

"On April 27, 2007 I bought 500 shares of WFMI at $47.28 and sold 5 May $45 ITM (In-The-Money) Calls for $3.31 netting $1646.72. I sold ITM Calls because I wanted to give myself some downside protection just in case WFMI again turned down. On May 2, 2007 after a small downturn I bought another 1000 shares at $45.95 and sold 10 May $45 Calls for $2.36. At this point it looked like the price had stabilized and an ATM Call would be successful.

"This time I was wrong. No one can bat 1000. A week later when the Department of Justice indicated that they would not approve the acquisition of Wild Oats the stock went down over $5. After looking at the financials of WFMI again I felt that this drop in share price was an over reaction to the news. So, I decided to wait and let the price come back. In a case like this, patience is important. WFMI was still expanding and indicated that it would prevail in the acquisition of Wild Oats."

"Professor, may I ask a question?" Tiffany was looking intently at the screen that still displayed Rob's transactions with WFMI.

"Sure Tiffany. Go ahead."

"Would you go over how to read those transactions? And why do you do it like that?"

"Yes, well I like to have an analysis of each stock in my portfolio. Each investment is unique. My first goal with any investment is to have a positive cash flow. My second goal is to have a *very* positive cash flow. When I make an investment I am buying something, so that is cash out. I show that as a negative balance in the second to last column. As I make money with the investment by selling options or having stock called, that's cash inflow, which eventually gives me a positive balance in the next to last column. The S in a row indicates the sale of an option. At the end of that row you can see the type and disposition of the option sale. For example the sale on April 27 and May 2 were Call options, which expired (CE). Expired means the option on expiration day was worthless. Additional Calls were sold on August 17. If the stock gets called this becomes a CA (Call assigned). Assigned means my shares were purchased by the option holder, in this case for $45.00 per share. Note that 300 shares were called on September 21, 2007 for $13,492.25. November calls were sold on the remaining 1200 shares. These were called with a cash inflow of $53980.10. The total gain was $8021.97, for a 11.88% gain in seven months."

"The message here is that with patience and staying with the strategy of selling Calls over and over an excellent return is very possible."

Nicholas walked over to Graham and held out his hand. "Thank you so much for your presentation. I'm sure our club will benefit. Our track record is actually pretty good despite having bought a few stocks at the wrong time. We can definitely see the value of your formulas."

"Thank you Nicholas. It's been my pleasure. Before I leave I would like to give you a note of caution. Let me show you one more example."

9

A Note of Caution

Sometimes when you innovate, you make mistakes. It is best to admit them quickly, and get on with improving your other innovations.

Steve Jobs

"I want to emphasize that no stock market system is fool proof. You have all been impressed with the return available by selling options.

"But there is always the clear and present danger that the stocks you have selected can go down and totally wipe out any profit you've made from selling options.

"A prime example of what can happen in the real world is the trade experience I had with ValuJet (VJET).

"On May 3, 1996 I purchased 2000 shares of VJET for $13.50 each and sold December 12.50 Calls for a premium of $3.375. It was a gain of 25% if expired and 19% if called out in seven months. On May 11, 1996 a ValuJet DC9 crashed into the Everglades in Florida with no survivors. The price of the stock was affected when all of ValuJet's planes were grounded. Since I had losses built into my plan, I took action on June 18, 1996 and closed out my Call options (bought them back) and sold the stock the next day. This is noted in line two of the table as CC for Closed Call.

"What started out to be a good trade turned into a sizable loss with no foreseeable warning. Tragic and unforeseen events will happen when least expected.

"I do everything I can to protect against stock market surprises.

"I keep this account summary with me as constant reminder of what can happen."

The following chart flashed on the TV screen.

VALUE JET					VJET	VJQ MAR JUN SEP DEC		
05-22-96	B		2000		13.500	27029.00	-27029.00	
05-22-96	S	20	DEC	12.50	3.375	6664.77	-20364.23	CC
06-18-96	B	20	DEC	12.50	.750	1550.00	-21914.23	
06-19-96	S		2000		6.625	13221.00	-8693.23	<

"But considering what transpired there is an important lesson to note. Anyone making this same investment without selling Calls would have had a greater loss by about $5100.

10

The Gift

Invest in companies, not stocks . . .
Peter Lynch

Jake was up early the next morning. After the professor's presentation to the investment club, and the gift, he was more motivated than ever to master the art of selling Covered Calls and Naked Puts.

The gift. Had it been a dream or was it real? It was definitely real. It was right in front of him and he was about to open it. But first he played over in his mind the events of the last evening.

The two men had left the investment club and were walking to their cars parked in a vacant lot about 200 feet from the Gardner home. Rob was silent. He was obviously considering something. Jake noticed and said nothing. There was a pleasant breeze from the gulf and Orion the Hunter was high in the night sky.

As they reached their cars the professor finally spoke. "Jake, do you remember our first session at the Yacht Club when I first began telling you about the money tree?"

Jake nodded.

"I slid a sheet of paper across the table for you to look at. I told you it was very simple but yet very powerful. Well, that was the first step and I've been very impressed with how much you have learned in the past two weeks. You've done your homework assignments. That first assignment required you to compute the percentage gain you would have with various options, both *If Expired* and *If Sold (Assigned)*. That was important because you needed to understand the very basics of options.

"This afternoon at the Yacht Club we talked about you building a prospect list. Like the manager of the Boston Red Sox you've got your first string that are in action competing for the pennant. But you also have many more players on the farm teams, in training and ready to go into action if called. Those are your prospects and you can have as many as you want.

"And in addition to building a prospect list you are ready to analyze your own portfolio based on the seven fundamental criteria and the Buy Rank that I covered tonight. This is a mammoth, potentially daunting, undertaking. You could easily get discouraged.

"So I have a gift for you."

With that Rob held out his hand, palm up. Lying in his hand was a small USB flash drive. Jake quickly picked it up and wondered just what he had.

"Tonight I demonstrated my Buy Limit and Buy Rank Wizard for the investment club. Also at the Rotary club presentation I demonstrated PIE, my Portfolio Income Explorer. What you have is more powerful and comprehensive. You have the VISIONS Stock Market Explorer. It includes PIE and the wizards, but much more.

"There are four key features that you will want to use as you begin picking dollars off your money tree.

"First, enter all the symbols for the stocks in your portfolio. VISIONS will search the market and prepare a table for you with the Buy Rank and the seven fundamental criteria for each stock. You can sort the list based on Buy Rank or any of the other columns. To make it even easier, one of the columns is called Best Fit. In this column a star rating is assigned to each stock based on how well it meets the seven fundamentals and the Buy Rank. The rating goes from no stars to four stars. Sorting by Best Fit will let you quickly identify quality. You will want to separate the gems from the duds.

"Second, easily build your prospect list, the players on your farm teams. Set a few key criteria and launch a VISIONS search of the entire stock market to find the several hundred stocks that are good prospects. These will also be presented to you in a table with Buy Rank, Best Fit and other values already computed.

"Third, using your portfolio as a base, launch the VISIONS Covered Calls search engine. You can specify minimum premium, expiration period and other criteria. For example, I usually search for Call premiums of 25 cents or greater and with expiration not greater than six months out. You can also, if you choose, specify ITM (In the Money Calls). VISIONS will bring back all the Call options for each of your stocks that meet the criteria you set. One of the columns gives a ranking of the premium based on how well they meet the requirements of the Magic Chart. That makes it easy to compare the value of a one-month option with a three-month option, and so forth. This column is similar to the Best Fit column for stocks. With options the best fit is a diamond and is identified by <->.

"Finally, fourth, you will want to launch the VISIONS Naked Puts search engine. The Put factor that I covered in our second session is automatically computed and you can sort the table by that value as well as others."

Jake looked down at his hand and noticed that his fingers had at some point in the last few minutes closed protectively around the flash drive. "Gosh, professor, this is just what I need. I feel like a guy digging a ditch in the hot sun with a shovel and I've just been presented a diesel, 400 horsepower backhoe with an air-conditioned cab."

"I know." Rob had turned towards the Bentley. "You will have fun with this. Good night."

And now it was morning. As usual he had enjoyed coffee and a bagel with Katie on the lanai. Their conversation was focused on the events of the evening before, but rushed, as Jake was eager to get into his home office. Now after getting another cup of coffee he entered his office, sat at his computer and inserted the flash drive.

11

Gems and Duds

*I get to play golf for a living. What more can you ask
for—getting paid for doing what you love.*

Tiger Woods

VISIONS opened. Jake took a few minutes to become familiar with the program which he had never seen before. From the opening page he found the input page that would allow VISIONS to search for data on his particular stocks.

There were currently 15 stocks in his portfolio. He entered the stock symbol for each and named the portfolio *Jake and Katie*. Soon the program was scouting the Internet for data on each of Jake's stocks.

As the program was running, Jake remembered he had not finished his bagel in his eagerness to explore VISIONS. He found the bagel and Katie still on the lanai.

"How's it going?" Katie asked.

"I've opened VISIONS and entered our stocks. The program is doing an analysis. We should have the results soon."

Taking a bite of his bagel Jake wandered back into his office. On the screen waiting for him was the VISIONS analysis of his portfolio.

VISIONS Search Results for Stock List [AAI, FLEX, NVLS, MOT, RHI, RSH, KLIC, AMR, TWX, MOLX, NTAP, CAH, MRVL, CPWR, TER, TOL, JBL, HD, AVID, QLGC, DOS, BC, CFL,....

Print Now Report Save Data Save Symbols Throw Away Set/Show Filters UnDo Sort Help Best Fit Key Help/Definitions Web Links BL/BR Wizard Data is Filtered

Company Name	Stock Symbol	Search Date	Quote	52Wk High	52Wk Low	50Day Avg	Buy Limit	Buy Rank	Best TA	I	Best Fit Beta	P/E	Div Ylds	Opn ?	Vol/ Day	Mkt Cap	Bare Cash	Rev/ Year	% Rev Gth/Y	Qtrly Erngs
MOTOROLA INC	MOT	07-04-08	7.06	19.68	7.06	8.73	10.21	9.98	GR		2.16	N/A	2.8	Y	24M	15B	-3B	34B	-21.0	-++-
EBAY INC	EBAY	07-04-08	26.80	40.73	25.10	29.12	29.00	5.63	GR	***	1.69	85.1	0	Y	13M	35B	638B	8B	24.00	++-+
INTEL CP	INTC	07-04-08	20.66	27.99	18.05	22.8	20.53	-0.54	TA	**	1.41	18.1	2.7	Y	55M	109B	3B	39B	9.3	++++
MICROSOFT CP	MSFT	07-04-08	25.98	37.50	23.19	28.17	26.76	2.18	TA	**	1.27	15.1	1.7	Y	69M	241B	17B	57B	0.4	++++
CISCO SYS INC	CSCO	07-04-08	23.12	34.24	21.77	25.46	24.88	5.64	GR	***	1.49	18.1	0	Y	50M	136B	12B	38B	10.4	++++
ALCOA INC	AA	07-04-08	32.78	48.77	26.69	39.25	32.21	-1.04	TA		1.28	12.7	2.1	Y	13M	26B	-6B	30B	-6.7	++++
GARMIN LTD	GRMN	07-04-08	41.95	125.68	39.75	46.30	61.23	8.97	GR	***	1.29	10.7	1.8	Y	4M	9B	37M	3B	34.9	++++
PENNEY J C CO	JCP	07-04-08	36.69	76.99	33.27	39.28	44.20	6.87	GR		1.07	8.3	2.2	Y	4M	8B	-1B	19B	-5.1	++++
HEWLETT PACKAR	HPQ	07-04-08	43.44	53.48	3999	46.10	43.36	-0.24	TA		1.00	14.1	0.7	Y	17M	107B	-4B	110B	10.7	++++
CATERPILLAR IN	CAT	07-04-08	70.31	87.00	59.60	79.93	66.45	-5.64	BI		1.02	12.6	2.4	Y	6M	43N	-17B	46B	17.8	++++
RADIOSHACK COR	RSH	07-04-08	12.26	34.98	11.58	13.75	17.43	8.83	BI		1.02	7.1	2.1	Y	4M	1B	-348M	4B	-4.4	++++
IMCLONE SYSTEM	IMCL	07-04-08	39.75	49.18	30.34	40.40	35.04	-10.01	BI		0.71	N/A	0	Y	1M	3B	-295M	611B	14.9	---+
APOLLO GP INC	APOL	07-04-08	55.18	81.68	37.92	48.36	48.86	-5.78	BI	*	0.62	27.6	0	Y	4M	9B	31M	2B	14.0	+--+
WALT DISNEY-DI	DIS	07-04-08	30.90	35.69	26.30	33.15	28.64	-9.63	BI		0.62	13.9	1.1	Y	12M	58B	-11B	37B	9.5	++++
WAL MART STORE	WMT	07-04-08	56.60	59.95	42.09	57.45	46.55	-22.51	BI		0.05	17.7	1.7	Y	19M	223B	-29B	387B	10.3	+++++

End Of List

"Wow! Katie, could you come in here."

As Katie came in Jake pointed to the screen. "Look, here's our portfolio. I'm just beginning to comprehend all that I'm seeing. But I think the key column is the Buy Rank column. The professor was explaining Buy Limit and Buy Rank last night at the investment club. It's a special formula the professor developed to determine if a stock is at the right point in its cycle to be a good prospect.

"Oh, but look at the far right column. Not all of our stocks had positive earnings for the last four quarters.

"I'm going to open the filter panel and click on the Buy Rank heading to sort the list by Buy Rank."

As Jake sorted by Buy Rank the following screen appeared. Katie pulled up a chair and they both continued analyzing.

VISIONS Search Results for Stock List [MOT,EBAY,INTC,MSFT,CSCO,AA,GRMN,JCP,HPQ,CAT,RSH,IMCL,APOL,DIS,WMT,....]

Print Now Report Save Data Save Symbols Throw Away Set/Show Filters UnDo Sort Help Best Fit Key Help/Definitions Web Links BL/BR Wizard Ready

Company Name	Stock Symbl	Search Date	Quote	52Wk High	52Wk Low	50Day Avg	Buy Limit	Buy Rank I	TA Best Fit	Best I	P/E	Beta	Div Ylds	Opn ?	Vol/ Day	Mkt Cap	Bare Cash Year	Rev/ Cash Year	% Rev Gth/Y	Qtrly Erngs
MOTOROLA INC	MOT	07-04-08	7.06	19.68	7.06	8.73	10.21	9.98	GR		N/1	2.16	2.8	Y	24M	15B	-7B	34B	-21.0	++++
GARMIN LTD	GRMN	07-04-08	41.95	125.68	39.75	46.30	61.23	8.97	GR	***	10.7	1.29	1.8	Y	4M	9B	-3B	3B	34.9	---
RADIOSHACK COR	RSH	07-04-08	12.26	34.98	11.58	13.75	17.43	8.83	GR		7.1	1.02	2.1	Y	4M	1B	76M	4B	-4.4	++++
PENNEY J C CO	JCP	07-04-08	36.69	76.99	33.27	39.28	44.20	6.87	GR		8.3	1.07	2.2	Y	4M	8B	-573M	19B	-5.1	++--
CISCO SYS INC	CSCO	07-04-08	23.12	34.34	21.77	25.46	24.88	5.64	GR	***	18.1	1.49	0	Y	50M	136B	767M	38B	10.4	++++
EBAY INC	EBAY	07-04-08	26.80	40.73	25.10	29.12	29.00	5.63	GR	***	85.1	1.69	0	Y	13M	35B	75M	8B	24.0	-+--
MICROSOFT CP	MSFT	07-04-08	25.98	37.50	23.19	28.17	26.76	2.18	TA	**	15.1	1.27	1.7	Y	69M	241B	327M	57B	0.4	++++
HEWLETT PACKAR	HPQ	07-04-08	43.44	53.48	39.99	46.10	43.46	-0.24	TA		14.1	1.41	0.7	Y	17M	107B	774M	110B	10.7	++++
INTEL CP	INTC	07-04-08	20.66	27.99	18.05	22.88	20.53	-0.53	TA	**	18.1	1.41	2.7	Y	55M	109B	1B	39B	9.3	++++
ALCOA INC	AA	07-04-08	32.78	48.77	26.69	39.25	32.31	-1.04	TA		12.7	1.28	2.1	Y	13M	25B	68M	30B	-6.7	++++
CATERPILLAR INC	CAT	07-04-08	70.31	87.00	59.60	79.93	66.45	-5.64	BI		12.6	1.02	2.4	Y	6M	43B	-725M	46B	17.8	++-+
APOLOO GP INC	APOL	07-04-08	55.18	81.68	37.92	48.36	48.86	-5.78	BI	*	27.6	0.62	0	Y	4M	9B	-3B	2B	14.0	++++
WALT DISNEY-DI	DIS	07-04-08	30.90	35.69	26.30	33.15	28.64	-9.63	BI		13.9	0.62	1.1	Y	2M	58B	56M	37B	9.5	++++
IMCLONE SYSTEM	IMCL	07-04-08	39.75	49.18	30.34	40.40	35.04	-10.01	BI		N/A	0.71	9	Y	1M	3B	107M	611M	14.9	++++
WAL MART STORE	WMT	07-04-08	56.60	59.95	42.09	57.45	46.55	-22.51	BI		17.7	0.05	1.7	Y	19M	223B	N/A	387B	10.3	++++

Visions Stock Filters [X]

Set these filters to the criteria for your search.

[A] [B] [C] [D] [E] [F]   [Get] [A] [Set] [v]

Select Favorite then Get to retrieve filter template.

Stock Symbols	Stock Price	Buy Rank (1)	TAI (1)	Best Fit (1)	Div Yield	Beta	Best Fit (1)	Bare Cash
Any	Any	Any	Any	Any	Any	Any	Any	Any

P/E Ratio	Options Req'd	Share Vol/Day	Rev/Year	Market Cap	Rev Grown/Yr	Qtrly Earnings
Any	Any	Any	Any	Any	Any	Any

[Do] [UnDo] [Set All to Any]   Help/Hints   [Hide]   # of Stock 15

After Filter selection, click on the yellow Do button. When the filtered data appears you can save the result or UnDo the filtering and try a new set of filters. Once the desired results are obtained you can save the filtered data (which includes the filters) to your storage bin. You can save the stock list to your prospect stock list file, or to your Call or Put Option stock list files. Updated your Favorite filter template at any time. When done select Throw Away above.

Copyright 2004 Groenke Software Engineering

Click here to add scroll bars to filter panel if needed

(1) From the book "Ca$h for LIFE" by Ronald Groenke Copyright 2006 ISBN 096741287O

"What's the Best Fit column?" asked Katie. "Some stocks have four stars and some have none."

Jake nodded. "Yes, I remember the professor talking about that last night. That may be the key to separating the gems from the duds. I think the more stars the better the stock matches the professor's seven fundamental criteria and the Buy Rank.

"But right now I'm eager to check out another feature of VISIONS. It's called PIE or Portfolio Income Explorer. The professor demonstrated it at the Rotary Club meeting when he was the speaker. Let's see if I can find it."

Katie went back to her computer as Jake continued working with VISIONS. Jake found the Run PIE button on the VISIONS Main Page and clicked on it. He soon called her back.

"Katie, come check this out."

The Portfolio Income Explorer results for their stocks appeared on the screen. Katie pulled up a chair and they both gazed silently at the screen for several moments.

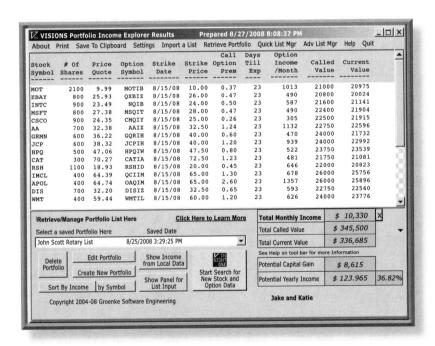

Katie was first to speak. "Jake, am I reading this right. You've been telling me about the Covered Calls money tree strategy. Does this income line, this $10,330, mean we can earn that much income just by selling options on our stock? Can that be true?

"Yes," Jake replied. "That's what it means. That is over $123,000 a year and I think we can do even better. Our portfolio is probably not the absolutely ideal selection of stocks for the money tree strategy. Only seven have a positive Buy Rank and ten don't have any stars in the Best Fit column.

"But now I want to see just what's out there. The professor said I would be able to search the entire stock market and find the real gems."

12

Building the Farm Teams

You may delay, but time will not.

Benjamin Franklin

"Jake, how about some lunch?"

Katie entered the office to find Jake still intently working with the VISIONS software program.

"Katie, my dear, this is just amazing. I've got to show you what I've learned. See this screen."

The first panel of Scout was on the computer screen.

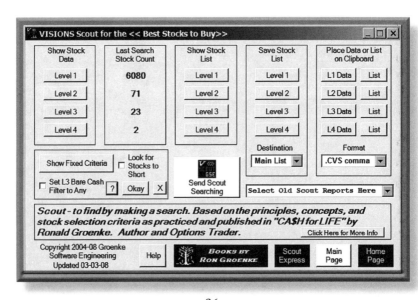

"Now all I have to do is set the criteria for stocks that I am interested in and then hit this button. There it's running. While VISIONS does its search let's go and have some lunch. How about we bike down to Vandy's for a salad?"

Ten minutes later they were pulling into the popular Marco Island restaurant. The waitress knew to fix Jake's salad with plenty of anchovies and of course none for Katie. Buttering a thick slice of homemade bread, Jake could not stop talking about his gift from the professor.

"Katie, I just can't get over the concepts and the practical application of the program. It's really very simple. You search the entire stock market, over 8,000 stocks, and then filter the list for those stocks that meet the professor's seven criteria or whatever criteria you want to set yourself.

"I'm sure I've still got a lot to learn. But it seems really simple. We will probably have several hundred stocks on our prospect list. I think maybe I should have stocks on the prospect list without regard to their Buy Rank because that's always changing as the stocks move through their up/down cycles. Then I will always be on the lookout for stocks that have the right Buy Rank.

"Oh gosh. I almost forgot. The professor said last night that VISIONS also has a search engine to find Calls and Puts. I can run that program for the stocks on my prospect list that have a good Buy Rank. Hmmm. Let's finish up. I'm anxious to get back."

As they parked their bikes and entered the house the phone was ringing. Katie answered the phone as Jake made a bee line for his computer. As he was experimenting with different ways of filtering his stock lists Katie came excitedly into the room.

"Jake, guess what. Never mind you'll never guess. That was Jean Graham on the phone. They've invited us over for lunch tomorrow. They have someone they want us to meet."

13

View from the Top

*In order to succeed, your desire for success should
be greater than your fear of failure.*

Bill Cosby

Jake and Katie had a panoramic view of Marco Island riding up the glass elevator to the Graham's penthouse condo. To their left was the Yacht Club at the foot of the Jolley Bridge, which connected the island to the mainland of southwest Florida. They spotted a small jet that had taken off from the Naples Airport, about 20 miles to the north. The pilot apparently wanted a birdseye view of Marco before his sharp turn north. Katie pointed out that they could see all the way to Goodland, a small fishing community on the south end of the island. Stan's Idle Hour Restaurant was a favorite in Goodland. The elevator was for the exclusive use of the two penthouse condos at the top of the most recent luxury tower built on the beach. As they stepped out onto the open foyer they had views of the beautiful crescent beach to the north and the south.

"I'm curious who they want us to meet," said Katie as Jake pushed the doorbell. Before the melodic chime had ended Jean Graham opened the door with a warm welcome.

"Come in," she smiled. "We are so glad you could come over. Rob has told me what a quick learner you are Jake. Oh Katie, what a beautiful sundress and how thoughtful of you to bring us these lovely flowers. Did you get them here on the island?"

"Yes, the Farmers Market on Wednesday has just about everything, including flowers. What a gorgeous condo," Katie replied.

Jean had the graceful movements of a ballerina as she welcomed Jake and Katie in.

"Jake, Rob is on the balcony waiting for you. There's a glass of ice tea for you out there. We'll join you in a moment."

Jake walked across the wide expanse of their "Great Room" to reach the balcony. The view outside was magnificent, but he was especially intrigued by the wide collection of paintings and artifacts. He quickly noticed items from the Orient, Australia and Europe. *World travelers*, he decided.

As he stepped out onto the balcony the sun was just high enough to begin casting its rays on the west balcony. The professor called from the corner to the north. "Come around here Jake. We can have the shade and still enjoy the view."

Jake settled in a comfortable lounge chair and picked up his iced tea as Rob set his book aside.

"We've always been so rushed in our prior meetings. Maybe this afternoon we can have a relaxing visit. You mentioned that you sold your CPA firm and moved to Marco to write a novel."

"Ah yes, the Great American Novel. I'm afraid that's just a crutch to keep from admitting that I'm finally retired. Although I think I do have an intriguing idea for a novel. But we get so involved with the kids and mainly the grandkids. Every time one graduates from middle school or high school we treat them to a major trip. This summer we are taking Sarah to Italy and Greece. That one-on-one time is really special. The novel? Well maybe some day."

"Yes. Jean and I do the same thing with the grandkids. They grow up so fast."

Rob stood up and looked out at the gulf and down the beach.

"Jake, would you bring the binoculars over. They are right there by your chair. Looks like a sail boat race is about to begin."

Jake joined Rob at the railing and they took turns looking at the sailboats in fierce competition about half way to the horizon. Looking down the beach they could see sunbathers and swimmers of all descriptions enjoying the surf. Just below them a volley ball game was in progress with six girls, on tour, playing against six local guys. The girl's team was in training for the summer Olympics and would no doubt handily defeat the local champions.

"Yes," Rob concluded his previous thought; "I enjoy focusing on my investments and spending time with Jean. We keep up with the kids and grandkids. What more does a man need in life?"

Jean and Katie joined them with a platter of sandwiches and pitcher of iced tea. "My specialty," said Jean. "Turkey on wheat with provolone cheese, lettuce, tomatoes and mayonnaise. I hope you like them."

Rob gave Katie a friendly hug. "So you are the reason my former student received a B instead of an A in Finance 101." They all laughed, enjoying the conversation along with the food.

Jean stood to take the plates from the table. "Is everyone ready for Key Lime pie? Why don't we move inside and be more comfortable."

As they began to move inside the doorbell chimed.

"Ah," said Rob. "That must be the person we want you to meet."

14

When to Take Action

Money never starts an idea; it is the idea that starts the money.

W. J. Cameron

Except for the long hair worn in a ponytail and the diamond stud in his left ear, the man looked like Rob Graham.

"Jake and Katie, meet my twin brother, Greg. Greg these are our friends, Jake and Katie Kimball."

As hands were being shook Rob continued. "Greg is a distinguished professor of mathematics in New Hampshire. He has been working on a formula that I think you will find interesting."

Greg's normally pale skin had taken on a Marco Island tan in the week he had been visiting. Jean brought coffee and key lime pie for everyone.

"Look at these incredible shells I found on Sand Dollar Island. And the birds. I can't get over it. You people actually live here. I'm just now beginning to relax. Soon I'll be back in the frozen north land."

As the group settled down, Katie was admiring a large oil painting on the wall. She had recently volunteered as a lecturer at the Naples Art Museum and had done in-depth research on renaissance paintings.

Leaning in Jean's direction she commented, "Jean, that painting is so familiar. But I can't decide on the artist. It is almost certainly from the late renaissance period. It has characteristics that you would find by da Vinci, Buonarroti or Raphael. But I can't name the painting."

Jean smiled. "I'll let Rob explain that."

Rob picked up his PDA and punched a few keys. The painting shimmered, seemed to come alive and then morphed into another equally dazzling late renaissance painting. To Katie the picture was again familiar but yet unique. She had never seen it before. Then the picture frame cleared and became a standard computer screen, 36 inches high by 64 inches wide.

"What you were looking at is a computer simulation," explained Rob. "We have a computer program that provides ambience based on who is in the room. When I am here alone the painting displayed, changing every hour, is a Salvador Dali, or rather a Salvador Dali if he were alive today. The program has analyzed all of Dali's paintings in the order that they were produced. It becomes, in effect, Dali and constantly produces new paintings. In similar fashion the computer has analyzed hundreds of renaissance paintings and provides a unique creation when we have guests.

"The program is based on a fuzzy logic concept and seems to be uncannily human at times. The simulated pictures often match my mood. Jean named the program HAL, and now it seems to respond better if called by that name. It responds to voice commands, but even without commands, it controls the ambience in the condo. For example it will adjust the lighting in a room if the TV is on. If the TV is off, you have plenty of light for reading wherever you happen to be. But when you leave the room the lights go off. It always knows who is where within the condo. Of course you can always override HAL with a voice command. At least so far," Rob concluded to a round of chuckles.

"But now let's get down to business. I've taken control of the monitor to more easily explain the break through that brother Greg has achieved. Greg has developed a formula that I believe will be very valuable.

"Jake, you know how important it is to pick the right stock. That's where I put my greatest emphasis. First, build a qualified prospect list. Then qualify the list with Buy Limit and Buy Rank formulas. And finally, you want to be sure the current price has crossed over the fifty day moving average."

"I understand," said Jake. "I could hardly go to bed last night. There are so many possibilities with VISIONS! It just blows me away!"

"Yes, I thought it might. But what I am about to show you is a quantum leap forward for the VISIONS program. All thanks to my dear brother Greg.

"Imagine that you could look at a stock chart and immediately know if it was Time to Take Action and sell a covered call or naked put that would prove successful. Imagine no more, for the answer is revealed here.

"Here's how it got started. There were many times when looking at a stock chart with a fifty-day moving average that I would notice that the current price was below the Buy Limit and the fifty-day average. The stock is a prime prospect, but the time for action is not quite here. How can I tell when it is time to act? I do not want to be too late but not too early either. I always felt there should be some way to combine the value of the Buy Rank with the fifty day moving average.

"I was inspired one evening when Jean and I were out walking and saw a shooting star, a small meteorite flashing across the earth's atmosphere. Some meteorites are reflected with a flash and others enter the atmosphere and display a burning tail as they near the earth. Why not develop a *Take Action Indicator* that signals when you should proceed with buying a stock and selling a Covered Call based on the current price approaching the buy limit and fifty-day moving average. As the price nears these values action should be taken. The challenge was putting the information into a formula that would give a reliable and consistent ranking.

"So when Greg came for a visit I knew he would soon be bored without a math challenge.

"OK. Greg why don't you explain your brilliant formula to Jake and Katie." Rob handed over the PDA.

"Glad to. Well, thanks to brother Rob, I've been supplementing my teaching income for the past year with options trading. In the back of my mind I kept thinking that there should be something more definitive than the Buy Rank for taking action. But I hadn't actually made the conceptual leap until Rob explained the objective.

"There is an ideal situation and then there is next best. The ideal situation is when the buy rank is greater than five, the fifty-day average is flat or increasing, and the current price has just crossed the fifty-day moving average.

"The next best is when the buy rank is positive and the current price is nearing or has just moved above the 50-day moving average. So here's the formula." Greg punched a few buttons and the following formula appeared on the screen.

$$TAI = 10 \times \frac{(CP) \times (CP) + 3 \times (FDA) \times (BL - CP) - (BL) \times (CP)}{(CP) \times (L - BL) + 2 \times (FDA) \times (BL - L)}$$

Greg continued as if it were the simplest thing in the world. "TAI stands for Take Action Indicator. CP is the current price of the stock that you are considering. FDA is the fifty-day moving average. BL is the Buy Limit and L is the fifty two week low."

With a look of utter despair Jake said, "Greg please. By the time I figure out this formula we'll be at the next expiration date. And if I do figure it out I may cause a nuclear explosion."

"Oh," replied Greg in a friendly jest. "Did you want the simple version? I think I can accommodate you," Greg said winking at his brother. "I did get it a little simpler. In this one, BR stands for Buy Rank."

$$TAI = BR \times \left(1 + \frac{FDA}{2 \times (FDA) - CP} \right)$$

Greg smiled, sipped his coffee and offered his favorite aphorism. "Continuous improvement allows one to sneak up on results that may have been previously viewed as unattainable."

"Greg should meet Lori Peterson," quipped Jake.

"What?"

"Oh, never mind. I'll explain later. I'm eager to see where you are going with this."

"Thanks Greg," said Rob reclaiming his PDA. "I've tried it out and so far it works great. Remember when looking at the buy rank by itself, I said anytime the Buy Rank was positive it was good and above five it was great. The take action indicator is a little different. We want to take action (Time to Act) when it is between 10 and—5, be cautious (Wait) when it is between—5 and—10, and look at other opportunities (Bad Idea) if it is less than—10. If the TAI has a value above 10 it may still be okay to proceed with this prospect, but a second review of the fifty-two week price chart with the fifty-day moving average is in order to see if the stock is still in a downward trend. We may be too early so we want to verify it (Get Ready) before we act."

"Here's what you are looking for on the TAI."

Rob wrote in his note pad and the following appeared on the screen.

"To get a better understanding of the Take Action Indicator I incorporated it into the VISIONS Stock Market Explorer software. With VISIONS this information is readily available on the stock data page and on the VISIONS chart. You can sort and filter your prospect stock data by TAI.

"Today's TAI is important, but how about a concept that gives you a view over time and provides additional guidance on when to act.

"The VISIONS View V is a window into how a stock is trading in relation to my Buy Limit and the 50 day moving average. It is truly unique and provides the information one needs to make better investment decisions. Here is how the VISIONS View V is constructed."

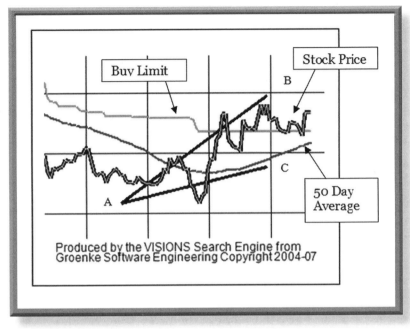

Point A is at the 52 Week Low.
Point B is at the Buy Limit plus .125 x (52 Week High - 52 Week Low).
Point C is at the 52 Week Low plus .125 x (52 Week High - 52 Week Low).

On the chart you can see how long the stock has been at each TAI value and be ready to take action once your stock prospect has traded in the VISIONS View V for a good number of days (20 is preferred). This makes it easy to decide which stock and option to add to your portfolio and which stocks in your portfolio you may want to sell."

"Here is a VISIONS chart that shows how Intel (INTC) had been in a Time to Act state for seventeen days and in the V for twenty three days on February 27, 2008.

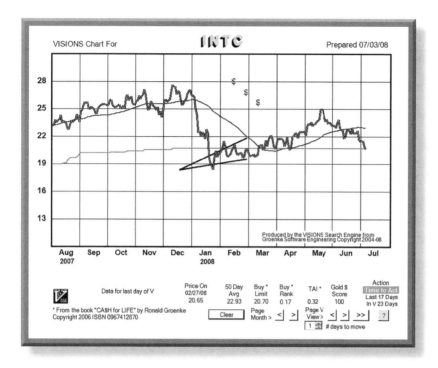

"The $ sign on the chart is a Gold $ sign inserted on the chart each day it is OK to instigate a trade. It attempts to show where the best trading opportunities are. The $ is shown when the GOLD $ Score is greater than or equal to the value that you feel is acceptable. A score of 100 is considered Ideal.

"On February 27, 2008 INTC had a Gold $ score of 100, which is considered Ideal. A three or four month OTM Covered Call would have been successful if executed at that time.

"The Score is calculated as follows:

"Ten times the number of up days plus two times the number of days the stock price is in VISIONS View V plus either 30 or zero. My formula adds 30 if the current stock price is in the V or within 5% of the 50-day moving average. Otherwise there is no addition.

"The Ideal case is when a stock is trading in the VISIONS V View for 20 days, going up the last 3 days, and within 5% of the 50-day moving average. The combination gives a perfect score of 100. This is, however, not fool proof. Make sure the fundamentals of the company meet your selection criteria before you act.

"Here is a graph of NTAP, which also indicated an ideal situation on February 27, 2008.

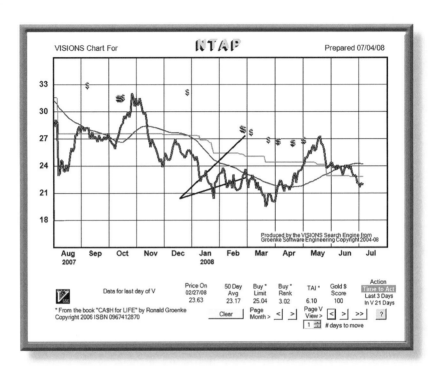

98

"Here is the chart for SYMC. This is one example that was shown to the investment club. When the club made their investment in SYMC the VISIONS View V indicated a Bad Idea for 30 days.

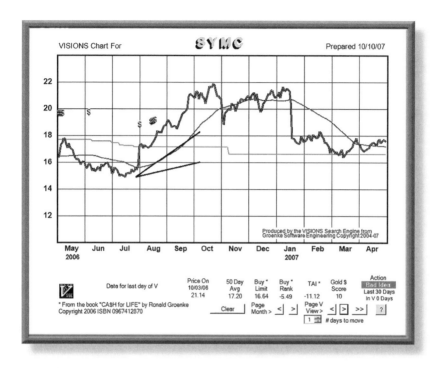

"On January 30, 2006 the VISIONS View V indicated a Time to Act for three days and a Gold $ score of 100 which is ideal. This is when I took action and executed a Covered Call. "

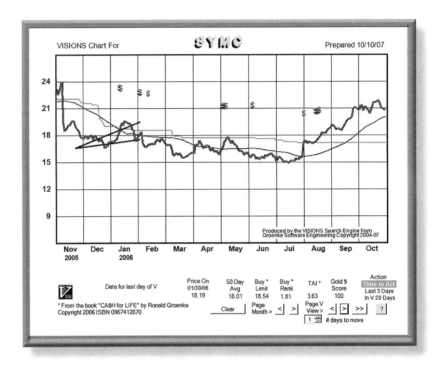

"Here again are the results of my trades."

SYMANTEC CORP					SYMC SYQ	JAN	APR	JUL	OCT
01-30-06	B		1300	18.22			23689.44	-23689.44	
01-30-06	S	13	APR	17.50	1.75		2129.93	-21559.51	CE
04-24-06	S	13	OCT	17.50	1.05		1345.20	-20214.31	CA
10-20-06	C		1300	17.50			22729.31	2515.00	<

Jake was beginning to get more excited. "Why, this takes all the hassle out of trying to figure out what to do and when to do it. With the VISIONS View V and Gold $ on the chart I am guided to the right stocks at the right time. And then with the call and put option search engines I can find the best calls and puts for each stock that meets the take action criteria. Wow!"

"Did you say you've incorporated this into your software?" asked Greg.

"Yes, it's all included in VISIONS. Like you said Jake, with the TAI, the VISIONS View V, and the Gold $, we now not only have a number but also a picture of when to act. This could give you the added advantage needed to improve the success rate for all your investments."

"Could we check another stock just to be sure I understand it? How about Garmin (GRMN). It's on my prospect list."

"Sure," Rob responded. "I will key-in GRMN for its current chart."

After a few seconds the following chart appeared.

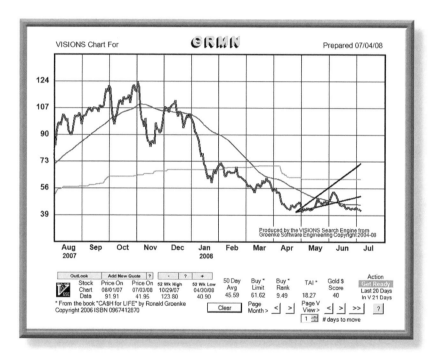

After quietly studying the chart for a few minutes Jake took a deep breath, exhaled slowly. "Well the Action indicator in the bottom right corner says "Get Ready" and it has been at this indication for 20 days. It also is not in the VISIONS V, so it may be premature to make an investment now."

"That's right," agreed Rob. "I would wait before making an investment in Garman at this point. You want to make sure the stock has established a lower support level. Having a little patience and waiting for it to move up into the V will improve your opportunity for a successful investment."

Rob closed his PDA and the screen became a live scene of a cabin on a lake. Icicles hung from the eves of the shuttered cabin and a cold rain was blowing across the frozen lake. Hearing the wind howl you could almost feel the brutal, teeth chattering deep freeze.

Looking at Greg the professor said, "HAL has a rather cruel sense of humor. I have a feeling that one is for you my brother."

Greg was staring even more intently at the screen. "You're not kidding. This is scary. That looks like Mount Moosilauke in the background. I can see it from my back deck at home. But how did HAL . . ." Greg's voice trailed off as the lights in the condo blinked twice.

15

Show Me the Money

Nine-tenths of wisdom is being wise in time.
Theodore Roosevelt

A glorious full moon was rising over the clear waters of the Caribbean. Jake and Katie enjoyed the view as they walked across the top deck of the cruise ship where they were to meet Rob and Jean. Over the past year they had practiced using VISIONS and were becoming masters of the art. Their portfolio, on which they sold Covered Calls had grown to 42 stocks. Their prospect list had several hundred stocks.

"Hurry, come look at the dolphins," Jean called to Jake and Katie from the port side of the deck. The dolphins seemed to be enjoying racing along with the fairly small luxury cruise ship. There were only 400 passengers and an equal number of staff and crew. The destination was Grand Cayman. But the whole purpose of the cruise was to provide an informal setting for the investment seminars sponsored by one of the major investment publications. Jake had written an article for the national magazine titled "The Professor's Money Tree" which resulted in Rob being invited to be one of the lecturers on the cruise.

"These are really posh accommodations," exclaimed Katie. "Now if I could just get these nautical terms right. Like how do you know which side is port and which side is starboard?"

"I heard a bit of trivia once that helps me with those terms, port and starboard," said Rob. "And it has to do with the word 'posh' that you just used Katie. When cruise ships first started going out of London down the coast of Europe and through the straits of Gibraltar, the first class passengers wanted to be on the side of the ship with a view of the coast. Naturally, they would be on the port or left side going down. Then on the return cruise home, they would change to the staterooms on the right or starboard side of the ship so they would still have a view of the coast. The term 'port out starboard home' or simply 'posh', became synonymous with first class accommodations."

Katie wrinkled her nose, which meant she was thinking about what she had just heard. "So you certainly wouldn't want SOPH accommodations. But I just noticed something interesting. I'll present it to you in the form of a question. What astronomical event always occurs with the rising of a full moon?"

Katie smiled, watching the perplexed looks. "Oh come on. It's not that difficult. It just occurred."

Jean was the first to get it. "Oh, I get it. I was a member of an astronomy club as a teenager. In order for the moon to be full it has to be directly opposite the sun. If it were not directly opposite the sun it would not be full. So, a full moon will rise just as the sun is setting, a very common astronomical event."

One of the staff came by with a tray of drinks and hors d'oeuvres. As they settled into lounge chairs Jake commented to Rob, "You really got a big response last night on your stock selection program. It seems most investors give lip service to *Buy Low, Sell High,* but think it's just a glib saying. And they were really amazed with the VISIONS V. I could tell that was a real eye opener for most of the audience. Many of them spend thousands of dollars for "expert" analysis. Now with your Stock Screener and VISIONS V they can search the entire market for those select stocks that meet important fundamental analysis and then find the ones approaching a possible up-cycle based on technical analysis.

"What will you talk about in tonight's lecture?"

Rob was thoughtful for a moment. "Stock investors fall into two categories, and many are in both. Some are most concerned with wealth preservation and others need income generation on a monthly basis. Of course, many investors have both objectives.

"Last night in the lecture on my stock selection criteria I was speaking primarily to wealth preservation. That is: How to pick stocks that have rock solid fundamentals and are poised for an up-cycle. Over the long haul, those stocks should have better appreciation than any random pick or index fund. "Tonight I will focus on monthly cash income. My topic is *Show Me the Money*. I want to demonstrate PIE. It rather dramatically demonstrates the power of my money tree approach to investing."

"Also, if we have time, I have a simulation of trades that is revealing. It speaks to an important question that was asked the first night in the opening session and which is typically not covered in these seminars. In fact, the guy made the point that he had read a lot of books about making money in the stock market. None of the systems he had read about ever took into account that the market goes down as well as up, that you can and do have real losses in the stock market. My software program simulates stock investments and the subsequent sell of Covered Calls. You can alter the various factors, including a stock loss, and see the resulting portfolio gain or loss over a period of time. My PDA works with the ships video system, so I can run the simulation based on questions from the audience in real time."

"What about the Cedric Chart? Are you going to show that?" Jake had been amazed at the apparent accuracy of the Buy/Sell time line chart of unknown origin, perhaps made as early as the Civil War.

"Hmmm. There are the fat years and the lean years. It might be interesting to get the reaction of this sophisticated group of investors."

Their conversation was interrupted by the familiar ship's bell that indicated the captain was about to make an announcement.

"This is the Captain speaking. Tonight's lecture by Dr. Robert Graham has been moved to the Main Theater to facilitate the increased demand. Dr. Charles Jackson's lecture on "Selecting the Right Mutual Fund" will now be held in Stateroom B."

* * *

Three seats had been reserved on the front row for Jake, Katie and Jean. Professor Graham walked immediately onto the stage and was introduced by Master of Ceremony, Steve Malcolm.

"Ladies and Gentlemen. Professor Graham will speak again tonight on his strategy of selling Covered Calls and Naked Puts. As you know, last night's topics, *The VISIONS V* and *Buy Low, Sell High,* have been the main topic of conversation all day. I'm sure that accounts for the overflow crowd tonight."

A murmur went through the audience. "I know some of you found last night's topic to be a little controversial, especially those of you associated with old line full service brokerage houses." The audience laughed, recalling the professor's blunt talk about the individual investor's ability to manage his own investment account. Steve winked at the Professor who smiled in return but otherwise maintained a professional decorum.

"Please welcome once again Professor Robert Graham."

The standing ovation surprised Graham. He quickly motioned for the audience to be seated so he could begin his presentation.

"Thank you," Rob said as he smiled warmly at the audience. He noticed the theater room was full and he could tell the investors were looking forward to more useful information.

"Last night in the seminar you saw the power of the VISIONS V to find stocks that have good fundamentals and are most likely to be at the beginning of an up-cycle. Tonight I want to move on to the crux of my investment strategy. Once you have good solid stocks in your portfolio, what then? Do you just hold for the long haul? Or is there a more proactive approach you can take?"

Professor Graham paused to let his questions sink in.

"Let's take a look at the possibilities. Most investors are familiar with the options market, but perhaps don't appreciate how powerful it can be for generating monthly income to increase your portfolio.

"Here's one quick example of how much income can be generated by selling stock options. I am using the top twenty revenue growth companies in the S&P 500 that also had positive earnings the last four quarters."

Rob flashed on the large screens the PIE results for the S&P 500 subset.

```
VISIONS Portfolio Income Explorer Results        Prepared 8/25/2008 3:59:326PM        _ |□| x|
About  Print  Save To Clipboard  Settings  Import a List  Retrieve Portfolio  Quick List Mgr  Adv List Mgr  Help  Quit
```

Stock Symbol	# Of Shares	Price Quote	Option Symbol	Strike Date	Strike Price	Call Option Prem	Days Till Exp	Option Income /Month	Called Value	Current Value
AAPL	100	176.79	APVIP	8/15/08	190.00	4.95	25	594	1800	17679
ADM	400	26.21	ADMIF	8/15/08	30.00	0.20	25	96	12000	10484
APA	100	111.57	APAIC	8/15/08	115.00	3.90	25	468	11500	11157
BK	300	34.39	BKIG	8/15/08	35.00	1.55	25	558	10500	10317
CVS	300	37.63	CVSIH	8/15/08	40.00	0.15	25	54	12000	11289
DVN	100	102.28	DVNIA	8/15/08	105.00	3.50	25	420	10500	10228
EOG	100	103.64	EOGIA	8/15/08	105.00	4.30	25	516	10500	10374
FCQ	200	90.60	FCXIS	8/15/08	95.00	3.40	25	816	19000	18120
GME	300	44.16	GMEII	8/15/08	45.00	1.75	25	630	13500	13248
HES	100	106.27	IGGIB	8/15/08	110.00	4.10	25	492	11000	10627
MRO	300	44.97	MROII	8/15/08	45.00	1.85	25	666	13500	13491
MUR	200	77.64	MURIP	8/15/08	80.00	2.30	25	552	16000	15528
NYX	300	41.14	NYXII	8/15/08	45.00	0.62	25	223	13500	12342
OXY	200	81.78	OXYIQ	8/15/08	85.00	1.95	25	468	17000	19356
PLD	300	44.33	PLDII	8/15/08	45.00	1.60	25	576	13500	13299
PPG	200	62.45	PPGIM	8/15/08	65.00	0.65	25	156	13000	12490
RIG	100	129.74	RIGIF	8/15/08	130.00	4.70	25	564	13000	12974
STT	200	66.95	STTIN	8/15/08	70.00	1.40	25	336	14000	13390
VLO	300	33.66	VLOIC	8/15/08	34.00	1.64	25	590	10200	10098
XTO	300	48.34	XTOIJ	8/15/08	50.00	1.65	25	594	15000	14502

```
Retrieve/Manage Portfolio List Here      Click Here to Learn More    Total Monthly Income    $ 9,370  |X|

Select a saved Portfolio Here           Saved Date                   Total Called Value      $ 267,200

    SP500 Top 20          8/25/2008 3:57:01 PM              ▼         Total Current Value     $ 257,983

                                                                     See Help on tool bar for more Information
  Delete        Edit Portfolio           Show Income      [PIE]
 Portfolio                               from Local Data           Potential Capital Gain    $ 9,217
              Create New Portfolio                   Start Search for
                                         Show Panel for  New Stock and  Potential Yearly Income $ 112,435   43.58%
  Sort By Income   by Symbol             List Input      Option Data

    Copyright 2004-08 Groenke Software Engineering              SP500 Top 20
```

Professor Graham gave the audience a minute to let the information on the large screens sink in. The audience seemed surprised to see the possibilities when income from selling Calls became apparent. The obvious question that everyone asked was: "I wonder how much income my portfolio would generate?" Hands were shooting up all over the theater wondering if they could check options on their stock portfolios.

Professor Graham raised both of his hands to quiet down the room.

"The monthly income of $9,370 is from the Covered Call option premium for the number of days until option expiration. Additional capital gains may be experienced if some of the positions are called. The yearly potential gain is over 43%. The options selected for each holding is provided along with the strike date, strike price and premium. PIE then shows the option income possible per month."

One man asked, "Dr. Graham, will your program, what did you call it?"

"PIE, Portfolio Income Explorer."

"Will PIE do this same analysis with any group of stocks?"

"Yes, PIE can be used with any list of stocks. It provides this same analysis. If you will give me your favorite stock I can demonstrate it now. "Let's take 25 stocks from the audience and see what the results are."

As the audience called out stocks the professor filled in a new input list for PIE and flashed the following on the screens:

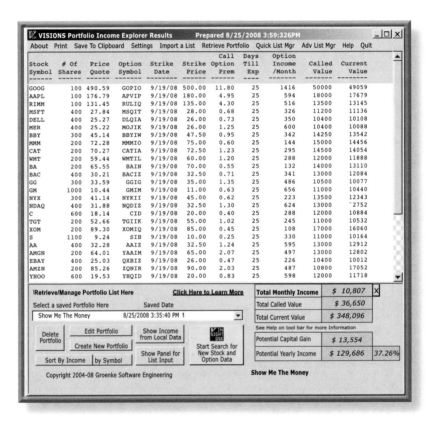

Stock Symbol	# Of Shares	Price Quote	Option Symbol	Strike Date	Strike Price	Call Option Prem	Days Till Exp	Option Income /Month	Called Value	Current Value
GOOG	100	490.59	GOPIO	9/19/08	500.00	11.80	25	1416	50000	49059
AAPL	100	176.79	APVIP	9/19/08	180.00	4.95	25	594	18000	17679
RIMM	100	131.45	RULIQ	9/19/08	135.00	4.30	25	516	13500	13145
MSFT	400	27.84	MSQIT	9/19/08	28.00	0.68	25	326	11200	11136
DELL	400	25.27	DLQIA	9/19/08	26.00	0.73	25	350	10400	10108
MER	400	25.22	MOJIK	9/19/08	26.00	1.25	25	600	10400	10088
BBY	300	45.14	BBYIW	9/19/08	47.50	0.95	25	342	14250	13542
MMM	200	72.28	MMMIO	9/19/08	75.00	0.60	25	144	15000	14456
CAT	200	70.27	CATIA	9/19/08	72.50	1.23	25	295	14500	14054
WMT	200	59.44	WMTIL	9/19/08	60.00	1.20	25	288	12000	11888
BA	200	65.55	BAIN	9/19/08	70.00	0.55	25	132	14000	13110
BAC	400	30.21	BACIZ	9/19/08	32.50	0.71	25	341	13000	12084
GG	300	33.59	GGIG	9/19/08	35.00	1.35	25	486	10500	10077
GM	1000	10.44	GMIM	9/19/08	11.00	0.63	25	656	11000	10440
NYX	300	41.14	NYKII	9/19/08	45.00	0.62	25	223	13500	12343
NDAQ	400	31.88	NQDIZ	9/19/08	32.50	1.30	25	624	13000	`2752
C	600	18.14	CID	9/19/08	20.00	0.40	25	288	12000	10884
TGT	200	52.66	TGIIK	9/19/08	55.00	1.02	25	245	11000	10532
XOM	200	89.30	XOMIQ	9/19/08	85.00	0.45	25	108	17000	16060
S	1100	9.24	SIB	9/19/08	10.00	0.25	25	330	11000	10164
AA	400	32.28	AAIZ	9/19/08	32.50	1.24	25	595	13000	12912
AMGN	200	64.01	YAAIM	9/19/08	65.00	2.07	25	497	13000	12802
EBAY	400	25.03	QXBIZ	9/19/08	26.00	0.47	25	226	10400	10012
AMZN	200	85.26	ZQNIR	9/19/08	90.00	2.03	25	487	10800	17052
YHOO	600	19.53	YHQID	9/19/08	20.00	0.83	25	598	12000	11718

VISIONS Portfolio Income Explorer Results   Prepared 8/25/2008 3:59:326PM

About Print Save To Clipboard Settings Import a List Retrieve Portfolio Quick List Mgr Adv List Mgr Help Quit

Retrieve/Manage Portfolio List Here   Click Here to Learn More

Select a saved Portfolio Here   Saved Date

Show Me The Money   8/25/2008 3:35:40 PM 1

Delete Portfolio Edit Portfolio Show Income from Local Data

Create New Portfolio

Sort By Income | by Symbol Show Panel for List Input Start Search for New Stock and Option Data

Total Monthly Income	$ 10,807
Total Called Value	$ 36,650
Total Current Value	$ 348,096
Potential Capital Gain	$ 13,554
Potential Yearly Income	$ 129,686	37.26%

See Help on tool bar for more Information

Copyright 2004-08 Groenke Software Engineering   Show Me The Money

"This list shows lower gains than the S&P 500 subset. It has stocks from many sectors, some which may even be depressed right now. But again the income possibilities are significant.

"This monthly cash income from selling Calls can be used any way you choose. It could supply enough for monthly living expenses or it could have a powerful compound growth effect on your portfolio.

"Now I want to show you a simulation of what can happen to your portfolio if you allow the income from selling Calls to be reinvested each month in additional stocks."

16

Despite Taxes
and Losses

It's not that I'm so smart, it's just that I stay with problems longer.
Albert Einstein

Rob continued. "By the way, as all of you I am sure are aware, some of your stock picks are bound to go bad. No matter how careful you are with the stock's fundamentals and technical analysis, we are dealing with a dynamic market. New competition with a technological innovation, bad management decisions, or an unknown number of events can cause a stock to suffer substantial losses. An accurate, honest simulation will have to take into account the certainty of some losses occurring in your portfolio.

"Now let's establish the parameters for our simulation. In most cases option values follow the normal ups and downs of the market, so let's be realistic in our expected gains. Is 20% possible? Is 30% possible? I'm saying yes. Is a 50% gain in one year on your investments with options is possible? I've been there, done that! Okay, what is realistic? Let's pick a goal of 25%. Would you agree that a 25% return on your stock portfolio would be pretty good?

"Let's keep it simple for illustration purposes. We are going to take

$25000 and buy three different stocks and sell Covered Calls. I personally like to have income coming in each month, so for the first month I will sell a one-month-out Call on one stock, a two-month -out Call on the second stock and a three-month-out Call on the third stock. We'll assume we are starting in January. In February and subsequent months we will sell three month Calls.

"We start the simulation with an initial investment of $25,000."

Rob punched the numbers into his PDA and the results flashed on the three large screens. "We need to make a couple of assumptions. First, how much premium as a percentage of the stock price could you expect to get for a three-month option? My experience has been that you can fairly easily get a 10% return for three months. You will need to test this yourself by checking the Call premiums on some of your favorite stocks. You can easily get this information from your online broker. Or go to www.yahoo.com. You may find it easier to get 4% for one month than 10% for three months. It all depends on stock volatility. The higher the stocks volatility, the greater the premium you receive. Anyway, for our simulation we will use 3.3% a month or 10% for three months.

"Now the next assumption is stock loss. Unless you are absolutely brilliant and extremely lucky, you will pick some stocks that insist on going down in value rather than up. I will use a 15% loss factor. The simulator will sell two of my stocks each year for a combined loss of 15% of the beginning of year portfolio value. Does that seem reasonable?"

There were sounds of agreement from the audience.

"Another factor we need to consider is the tax effect. At the end of each year I have the simulation deduct 25% of the net income—Call premiums less stock losses—from the portfolio to keep the tax man happy. For simplicity I have ignored commission expense and gains from stock appreciation. Commissions are low if you use a good online broker and would be more than off set by gains from stock appreciation on OTM Calls. Also, in this particular simulation, we are not using the leverage available in margin accounts."

SIMULATION SETUP SUMMARY
PORTFOLIO GROWTH
THROUGH THE SELLING OF
COVERED CALLS FACTORS:

1. INITIAL INVESTMENT: $25,000
2. 10% PREMIUM PER QUARTER
   (3.3% PER MONTH)
3. ASSUMED STOCK LOSSES EACH YEAR OF 15%
   OF BEGINNING BALANCE
4. ASSUMED TAX OF 25% OF NET INCOME
   (PREMIUMS LESS LOSSES)

In the Illustrator the following was shown on the screens:

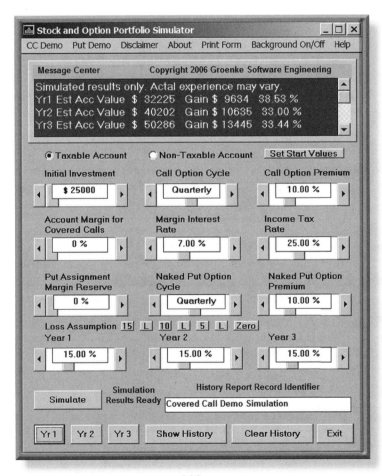

"OK. Here comes the simulation for the first six months."

YEAR ONE

MONTH	TRANSACTION	AMT	BAL	INC
JAN	INITIAL INVESTMENT	25000	25000	
	BUY A & SELL MAR CALLS	−12500	12500	
	OPTIONS SOLD AT 6.7 %	837	13337	
	BUY B & SELL APR CALLS	−10670	2667	
	OPTIONS SOLD AT 10 %	1067	3734	
	BUY C & SELL FEB CALLS	− 3734	-0-	
	OPTIONS SOLD AT 3.3 %	123	123	
	OPTION PREM INCOME JAN			2027
FEB	STK C CALLED OR EXPIRED	3734	3857	
	STK C SELL MAY CALLS	− 3857	-0-	
	OPTIONS SOLD AT 10 %	385	385	
	OPTION PREM INCOME FEB			385
MAR	STK A CALLED OR EXPIRED	12500	12885	
	STK A SELL JUN CALLS	12885	-0-	
	OPTIONS SOLD AT 10 %	1288	1288	
	OPTION PREM INCOME MAR			1288
APR	STK B CALLED OR EXPIRED	10670	11958	
	STK B SELL JUL CALLS	11958	-0-	
	OPTIONS SOLD AT 10 %	1195	1195	
	OPTION PREM INCOME APR			1195
MAY	STK C CALLED OR EXPIRED STK C	3857	5053	
	SELL AUG CALLS	−5053	-0-	
	OPTIONS SOLD AT 10 %	505	505	
	OPTION PREM INCOME MAY			505
JUNE	STK A CALLED OR EXPIRED	12885	13391	
	STK A SELL SEP CALLS	-13391	-0-	
	OPTIONS SOLD AT 10 %	1339	1339	
	OPTION PREM INCOME JUN			1339

"Let's go over the first six months. In January we make an initial investment in our brokerage account of $25,000. We buy three stocks, A, B and C, selected from our prospect list. As you recall last night, I talked briefly about my system of ranking stocks and use of the TAI formula. Stock selection is very important, but in tonight's discussion we are focusing on the three-year simulation.

"For our first purchase of stock A, we sell March Calls (two months out) for a premium of 6.7%. For simplicity we are assuming the strike price is the same as the purchase price when in reality the strike price would frequently be about 5% to 10% above the purchase price.

"The $837 premium received is added to our account balance and used in the purchase of stocks B & C. Thus the compounding effect begins in the very first month. On stock B, we sell April Calls (three months out) and on stock C we sell February Calls (one month out). In the following months all Calls will be for three months. By staggering the Calls the first month and then selling three-month options we are able to have premium income each month.

"Each stock will either be called and will receive cash or the option will expire. Either event leaves us in position to repeat the process of selling additional Calls on the same stock and keeping or reinvesting the premium received.

"Now let's take a look at the last six months portfolio value at year's end."

MONTH	TRANSACTION	AMT	BAL	INC
JULY	STK B CALLED OR EXPIRED	11958	13297	
	STK B SELL OCT CALLS	-13297	-0-	
	OPTIONS SOLD AT 10 %	1329	1329	
	OPTION PREM INCOME JUL			1329
AUG	STK C CALLED OR EXPIRED	5053	6383	
	STK C SELL NOV CALLS	-6383	-0-	
	OPTIONS SOLD AT 10 %	638	638	
	OPTION PREM INCOME AUG			638
SEP	STK A SOLD AT LOSS (13391 – 1500)	11891	12529	
	NEW A SELL DEC CALLS	-10023	2505	
	OPTIONS SOLD AT 10 %	1002	3508	
	BUY D SELL DEC CALLS	-3508	-0-	
	OPTIONS SOLD AT 10 %	350	350	
	OPTION PREM INCOME SEP			1353
OCT	STK B SOLD AT LOSS (13297 – 2250)	11047	11398	
	NEW B SELL JAN CALLS	-11398	-0-	
	OPTIONS SOLD AT 10 %	1139	1139	
	OPTION PREM INCOME OCT			1139

NOV	STK C CALLED OR EXPIRED	6383	7523	
	STK C SELL FEB CALLS	-7523	-0-	
	OPTIONS SOLD AT 10 %	752	752	
	OPTION PREM INCOME NOV			752
DEC	A&D CALLED OR EXPIRED	13531	14284	
	STK A&D SELL MAR CALLS	-14284	-0-	
	OPTIONS SOLD AT 10 %	1428	1428	
	TAX RESERVE	-2408	-980	
	OPTION PREM INCOME DEC			1428
TOTAL PREMIUM INCOME YEAR ONE				13378

PORTFOLIO VALUE AT YEAR END		
	AMT	BALANCE
STOCK A & D	14284	14284
STOCK B	11398	25682
STOCK C	7523	33205
CASH (DEC PREMIUMS)	1428	34633
25% TAX ON NET INCOME (PREMIUMS LESS LOSSES)	-2408	32225
ASSUMED STOCK LOSSES		3750
GAIN AFTER TAX & LOSS		7225
RETURN ON INVESTMENT		28.90%

"Notice the transactions in September and October. In those months we incur stock market losses of $1500 and $2250, 15% of the beginning of year portfolio balance. These losses reflect real life experiences. No matter how careful you are, there will be stock market losses. For simulation purposes we have just assumed we will lose 15% each year. These losses could occur because the stock price went down and we decided to sell the stock. Perhaps the stock no longer meets our stock selection criteria such as profitable quarters or volume of trades. Another way we could experience a loss is when the market price goes down and we decide to sell Calls at a lower strike price than our original purchase price. If that happens, and the stock is called, we again have a stock loss. In that case the loss may well be offset by premium income, but it is still a loss. A stock market strategy is only worthwhile if it can overcome those losses and still show a significant gain.

"Notice in December we deduct $2,408 for tax reserve. This is 25% of net income, $13,378 premium income less the $3,750 stock losses.

"Taxes are even more certain than stock market losses. It's best to just accept the fact that you are going to make money and you will need to pay taxes. As the quantity of premium income increases, you will probably need to make quarterly payments to the IRS. Plan ahead. Set aside a reserve so you aren't caught in a situation of having to liquidate some investments to pay taxes.

"Finally, how did we do for the year? Even after taxes and market losses our portfolio value has grown to $32,225 from selling Call options. We are ignoring the possibility of stock market appreciation.

"Our portfolio growth of $7,225 represents a return on investment of 28.9%."

"Now we move on to year two."

Professor Graham flashed all of year two and the summary onto the screens.

YEAR TWO

MONTH	TRANSACTION	AMT	BAL	INC
JAN	BALANCE FORWARD		-980	
	STK B CALLED OR EXPIRED	11398	10418	
	STK B SELL APR CALLS	-10418	-0-	
	OPTIONS SOLD AT 10 %	1041	1041	
	OPTION PREM INCOME JAN			1041
FEB	STK C CALLED OR EXPIRED	7523	8565	
	STK C SELL MAY CALLS	- 8565	-0-	
	OPTIONS SOLD AT 10 %	856	856	
	OPTION PREM INCOME FEB			856
MAR	A&D CALLED OR EXPIRED	14284	15140	
	STK A SELL JUN CALLS	7570	7570	
	OPTIONS SOLD AT 10 %	757	8327	
	STK D SELL JUN CALLS	8327	-0-	
	OPTIONS SOLD AT 10 %	833	833	
	OPTION PREM INCOME MAR			1590

APR	STK B SOLD AT A LOSS (10418 – 1450) STK B SELL JUL CALLS OPTIONS SOLD AT 10 % OPTION PREM INCOME APR	8968 -9801 980	9801 -0- 980	980
MAY	STK C CALLED OR EXPIRED STK C SELL AUG CALLS OPTIONS SOLD AT 10 % OPTION PREM INCOME MAY	8565 -9545 954	9545 -0- 954	954
JUNE	A & D CALLED OR EXPIRED STK A SELL SEP CALLS OPTIONS SOLD AT 10 % STK D SELL SEP CALLS OPTIONS SOLD AT 10 % OPTION PREM INCOME JUNE	15897 -8426 843 -9269 927	16852 8426 9269 -0- 927	1770
JULY	STK B CALLED OR EXPIRED STK B SELL OCT CALLS OPTIONS SOLD AT 10 % OPTION PREM INCOME JUL	9801 -10728 1072	10728 -0- 1072	1072
AUG	STK C CALLED OR EXPIRED STK C SELL NOV CALLS OPTIONS SOLD AT 10 % OPTION PREM INCOME AUG	9545 -10617 1062	10617 -0- 1062	1062
SEP	A&D CALLED OR EXPIRED NEW A SELL DEC CALLS OPTIONS SOLD AT 10 % NEW D SELL DEC CALLS OPTIONS SOLD AT 10 % OPTION PREM INCOME SEP	17695 9378 938 10316 1031	18757 9378 10316 -0- 1031	1969
OCT	STK B CALLED OR EXPIRED STK B SELL JAN CALLS OPTIONS SOLD AT 10 % OPTION PREM INCOME OCT	10728 11759 1176	11759 -0- 1176	1176
NOV	STK C SOLD AT A LOSS (10617 - 3384) STK C SELL FEB CALLS OPTIONS SOLD AT 10 % OPTION PREM INCOME NOV	7234 -8410 841	8410 -0- 841	841

Continued on next page

Continued from previous page

	A&D CALLED OR EXPIRED	19694	20535		
	NEW A SELL MAR CALLS	10268	10267		
	OPTIONS SOLD AT 10 %	1027	11294		
DEC	NEW D SELL MAR CALLS	11294	-0-		
	OPTIONS SOLD AT 10 %	1129	1129		
	TAX RESERVE	2659	-1530		
	OPTION PREM INCOME DEC			2156	
TOTAL PREMIUM INCOME YEAR TWO				15467	

PORTFOLIO VALUE AT YEAR END		
	AMT	BALANCE
STOCK A	10268	10268
STOCK B	11759	22027
STOCK C	8410	30437
STOCK D	11295	41732
CASH	1129	42861
25% TAX ON NET INCOME (PREMIUMS LESS LOSSES)	-2659	40202
ASSUMED STOCK LOSSES		4834
GAIN AFTER TAX & LOSS		7977
RETURN ON INVESTMENT		24.75%

"The key point here is that the advantages of compounding are powerful, but begin slowly. Our portfolio has grown by almost $8,000 or 24.75%. Accordingly, we have larger stock losses and reserve for taxes.

"Let's go on to year three."

YEAR THREE

MONTH	TRANSACTION	AMT	BAL	INC
JAN	BALANCE FORWARD B CALLED OR EXPIRED STK B SELL APR CALLS OPTIONS SOLD AT 10 % OPTION PREM INCOME APR	 11759 -10229 1023	-1530 10229 -0- 1023	 1023
FEB	STK C CALLED OR EXPIRED STK C SELL MAY CALLS OPTIONS SOLD AT 10 % OPTION PREM INCOME FEB	8410 - 9433 943	9433 -0- 943	 943
MAR	A&D CALLED OR EXPIRED STK A SELL JUN CALLS OPTIONS SOLD AT 10 % STK D SELL JUN CALLS OPTIONS SOLD AT 10 % NEW E SELL JUN CALLS OPTIONS SOLD AT 10 % OPTION PREM INCOME MAR	21562 11253 1125 -9902 990 -3465 346	22505 11252 12377 2475 3465 -0- 346	 2462
APR	STK B CALLED OR EXPIRED STK B SELL JUL CALLS OPTIONS SOLD AT 10 % OPTION PREM INCOME APR	10230 -10576 1057	10576 -0- 1057	 1057
MAY	STK C CALLED OR EXPIRED STK C SELL AUG CALLS OPTIONS SOLD AT 10 % OPTION PREM INCOME MAY	9433 -10490 1049	10490 -0- 1049	 1049
JUNE	A&D CALLED OR EXPIRED STK A SELL SEP CALLS OPTIONS SOLD AT 10 % STK D SELL SEP CALLS OPTIONS SOLD AT 10 % STK E SELL SEP CALLS OPTIONS SOLD AT 10 % OPTION PREM INCOME JUN	24621 -12835 1283 -11295 1129 -3953 395	25670 12835 14118 2824 3953 -0- 395	 2808
JULY	STK B SOLD AT LOSS (10756 – 3015) NEW B SELL OCT CALLS OPTIONS SOLD AT 10 % OPTION PREM INCOME JUL	 7561 -7956 795	 7956 -0- 795	 795

Continued on next page

Continued from previous page

AUG	STK C CALLED OR EXPIRED	10491	11286	
	STK C SELL NOV CALLS	-11286	-0-	
	OPTIONS SOLD AT 10 %	1128	1128	
	OPTION PREM INCOME AUG			1128
SEP	STK D SOLD AT LOSS			
	(11295 – 3015)	8280	9408	
	NEW D SELL DEC CALLS	-6706	2702	
	OPTIONS SOLD AT 10 %	670	3372	
	A&E CALLED OR EXPIRED	16788	20160	
	STK A SELL DEC CALLS	-10478	9682	
	OPTIONS SOLD AT 10 %	1048	10730	
	STK E SELL DEC CALLS	-8584	2146	
	OPTIONS SOLD AT 10 %	858	3004	
	NEW F SELL DEC CALLS	-3004	-0-	
	OPTIONS SOLD AT 10 %	300	300	
	OPTION PREM INCOME SEP			2876
OCT	STK B CALLEDOR EXPIRED	7957	8257	
	STK B SELL JAN CALLS	-8257	-0-	
	OPTIONS SOLD AT 10 %	826	826	
	OPTION PREM INCOME OCT			826
NOV	STK C CALLEDOR EXPIRED	11286	12112	
	STK C SELL FEB CALLS	-12112	-0-	
	OPTIONS SOLD AT 10 %	1211	1211	
	OPTION PREM INCOME NOV			1211
DEC	A,D,E&F CALLED	28773	29984	
	NEW A SELL MAR CALLS	-11994	17990	
	OPTIONS SOLD AT 10 %	1199	19190	
	NEW D SELL MAR CALLS	-7676	11514	
	OPTIONS SOLD AT 10 %	768	12282	
	STK E SELL MAR CALLS	-9825	2456	
	OPTIONS SOLD AT 10 %	982	3438	
	STK F SELL MAR CALLS	-3438	-0-	
	OPTIONS SOLD AT 10 %	343	343	
	TAX RESERVE	3361	–3018	
	OPTION PREM INCOME DEC			3292
TOTAL PREMIUM INCOME YEAR THREE				19470

PORTFOLIO VALUE AT YEAR END	AMT	BALANCE
STOCK A	11994	11994
STOCK B	8257	20251
STOCK C	12112	32363
STOCK D	7676	40039
STOCK E	9825	49864
STOCK F	3438	53302
CASH	343	53645
25% TAX ON NET INCOME (PREMIUMS LESS LOSSES)	-3361	50284
ASSUMED STOCK LOSSES		6030
GAIN AFTER TAX & LOSS		10082
RETURN ON INVESTMENT		25.07%

"At the end of year three the portfolio has grown and we have diversified. We began with only three stocks and now have six. Of course, in real life, further diversification is possible and desirable.

"In three years we have doubled our portfolio from $25,000 to $50,000. The compounding effect is just beginning to take effect. In another three years the portfolio can grow to $100,000. After 10 years we could grow the $25,000 to $250,000 based on our assumptions of the 10% premium for three months, 25% tax and 15% stock market losses."

Steve Malcolm, the host and moderator, walked back on stage and shook hands with Professor Graham as the audience burst into an appreciative round of applause.

"Professor, I have a few questions from the audience if you don't mind," said Malcolm.

"Question one: For self directed IRA's and other retirement plans on which taxes are deferred, what would be the simulated result without taxes?"

Graham punched some numbers into his PDA and the following table flashed on the screens.

"I have run the simulation with different factors. If you avoid tax, as with a retirement account, and all other factors are the same as the simulation we just demonstrated, then the $25,000 grows to $61,540 in three years. Here are some interesting scenarios, beginning with the one demonstrated in detail tonight.

"The premium percentage is the Call option premium divided by its underlying stock cost for the cycle indicated. For the last three simulations, using funds borrowed from the brokerage account, an interest rate of 7% is factored in as an expense."

COVERED CALL SIMULATION RESULTS						
Initial Invest.	Prem.	Cycle	Margin	Loss	Tax	3 YR Result
$25,000	10%	Quarterly	-0-	15%	25%	$50,284
$25,000	10%	Quarterly	-0-	15%	-0-	$61,540
$25,000	3%	Monthly	-0-	15%	-0-	$49,507
$25,000	4%	Monthly	40%	15%	25%	$73,406
$25,000	8%	Quarterly	40%	15%	25%	$48,965
$25,000	10%	Quarterly	40%	15%	25%	$62,861

"Next question: what about Puts? The simulation only used Covered Calls."

"In my personal portfolio I use a strategy that combines both Calls and Puts to optimize return. For the beginning options investor I strongly recommend sticking with Covered Calls until you have gained experience.

"The simulation model allows you to include a certain level of Put activity along with your Covered Calls. If we allow, for example, 40% of our margin to be used to cover the addition of Naked Puts to the previous simulation, the account balance after three years is $71,617 instead of the $50,284 shown. This additional gain is from selling Puts and using the premium to invest in more Covered Calls.

"There are many combinations of Calls and Puts that one can consider. That is why the Stock and Option Portfolio Simulation software module is one of the most valuable tools to own since it makes all those what ifs understandable."

Malcolm was about to thank the Professor for a splendid presentation when a questioner interrupted them.

"Professor Graham," the man shouted. "I must ask one more question."

Malcolm glanced at Professor Graham who nodded consent.

The man began, "Look, I don't mean to be disrespectful. But I've been to many of these seminars. It always sounds good and I get all hyped up. But it's all just theory. And I get lost trying to put the theory into practice. You seem sincere. But how can I be sure?"

Professor Graham wanted to end the seminar on a positive note. He thought for a moment and said, "Would it help if I showed you some of my personal trading results?"

17

Trade Results

If a man has money, it is usually a sign, too, that he knows how to take care of it; don't imagine his money is easy to get simply because he has plenty of it.

Edgar Watson Howe

Professor Graham punched numbers in his PDA to prepare view graphs for the large screens in the auditorium.

"I have put together a Score Board of a number of my stock portfolios which I refer to as Score Cards. Each Score Card shows the trades made in the portfolio with a performance summary and a history of the trades for each stock. The Score Board summarizes the results of all the Score Cards. I also make these available on my website."

"Here is a sample Score Board for five Score Cards. These are provided as examples and not as recommendations."

VISIONS SCOREBOARD - A SUMMARY OF SCORECARD EXAMPLES AS OF 06-25-08					
SCORECARD	1	2	3	4	5
INITIAL INVESTMENT	60000	50000	200000	60000	50000
CALLED VALUE	96939	87440	212816	109670	34210
CASH BALANCE	3152	2455	3026	2726	6879
MARGIN EXPENSE	0	0	0	0	206
CASH WITHDRAWN	0	0	72000	0	0
OVERALL VALUE	100092	89895	287843	112396	40884
GAIN	40092	39895	87843	52396	-9115
%	66.82	79.79	43.92	87.32	-18.23
PERIOD (MONTHS)	24	38	37	33	45
ANNUALIZED GAIN	33.36	25.20	14.28	31.80	-4.86

"Of course, these results change every month after option expirations on the third Friday.

"Here is Score Card 1.

Scorecard # 1

```
VISIONS SEARCH ENGINES INVESTMENT EXAMPLE HISTORY           SCORECARD #1

THIS EXAMPLE IS BEING UPDATED OVER TIME TO SHOW WHAT IS POSSIBLE BY USING
THE FEATURES OF THE VISIONS SOFTWARE TO IMPLEMENT THE CONCEPTS IN THE BOOK
SHOW ME THE MONEY by RONALD GROENKE (ISBN # 978-I-9340020-8-7).

THIS EXAMPLE IS FOR LEARNING PURPOSES ONLY. IT IS NOT A RECOMMENDATION.

INVESTMENT PLAN SUMMARY                                        06-25-08

DATE      TRANSACTION                             (+/- AMOUNT)      BALANCE
--------  -------------------------------------   ------------   -----------
08-14-06  INITIAL INVESTMENT                      +   60000.00     60000.00

08-14-06  BOUGHT 1200 COMVERSE TECH     @ 19.900  -   23885.00     36115.00
          SOLD 12  CMVT JAN 20.00 CALLS @ 2.5500  +    3044.95     39159.95
          CALLED VALUE = 23980.20   SOLD % = 13.14  EXP % = 12.74

08-14-06  SOLD 10  CMVT JAN 15.00  PUTS @  .5000  +     484.98     39644.93

08-14-06  BOUGHT 1200 ALTERA CORP       @ 17.810  -   21377.00     18267.93
          SOLD 12  ALTR DEC 17.50 CALLS @ 1.8000  +    2144.96     20412.89
          CALLED VALUE = 20980.30   SOLD % =  8.17  EXP % = 10.03

08-14-06  BOUGHT 700  ROWAN COS INC     @ 32.210  -   22552.00     -2139.11
          SOLD  7   RDC OCT 32.50 CALLS @ 2.3500  +    1629.97      -509.14
          CALLED VALUE = 22730.24   SOLD % =  8.01  EXP % =  7.22

08-14-06  SOLD  5   RDC OCT 30.00  PUTS @ 1.3500  +     659.97       150.83

10-23-06  SOLD  7   RDC JAN 32.50 CALLS @ 2.5000  +    1734.94      1885.77
10-23-06  SOLD  6   RDC JAN 27.50  PUTS @  .8500  +     494.98      2380.75

12-15-06  1200 ALTR CALLED @ 17.50                +   20980.30     23361.05
12-18-06  BOUGHT 2500 TELLABS INC       @ 10.570  -   26430.00     -3068.95
          SOLD 25  TLAB JUN 10.00 CALLS @ 1.6000  +    3976.18       907.23
          CALLED VALUE = 24980.16   SOLD % =  9.55  EXP % = 15.04

01-22-07  BUY 100 RDC @ 31.51                     -    3156.00     -2248.77
01-22-07  SOLD  8   RDC APR 32.50 CALLS @ 2.0000  +    1584.94      -663.83
01-22-07  SOLD 12  CMVT APR 20.00 CALLS @ 1.2500  +    1484.95       821.12
01-22-07  SOLD  7   RDC APR 27.50  PUTS @  .7000  +     474.98      1296.10
01-22-07  SOLD 10   AMD APR 16.00  PUTS @  .7000  +     684.97      1981.07

04-20-07  1200 CMVT CALLED @ 20.00                +   23980.20     25961.27
04-20-07  800  RDC  CALLED @ 32.50                +   25980.13     51941.40
04-20-07  BUY  10   AMD APR 16.00  PUTS @ 1.8500  -    1865.00     50076.40
04-20-07  SOLD 13   AMD JUL 15.00  PUTS @ 1.5000  +    1934.93     52011.33
04-23-07  BOUGHT 1100 GOLD CORP         @ 25.650  -   28220.00     23791.33
          SOLD 11    GG JUL 25.00 CALLS @ 2.2500  +    2459.96     26251.29
          CALLED VALUE = 27480.08   SOLD % =  6.09  EXP % =  8.71
```

Scorecard # 1 *(continued)*

DATE	TRANSACTION	(+/- AMOUNT)	BALANCE
04-23-07	SOLD 8 GG JUL 22.50 PUTS @ .4500	+ 344.98	26596.27
04-23-07	BOUGHT 1100 SRA INTL @ 25.170	− 27692.00	-1095.73
	SOLD 11 SRX JUN 25.00 CALLS @ 1.3500	+ 1469.97	374.24
	CALLED VALUE = 27480.08 SOLD % = 4.54 EXP % = 5.30		
06-15-07	2500 TLAB CALLED @ 10.00	+ 24980.16	25354.40
06-15-07	1100 SRX CALLED @ 25.00	+ 27480.08	52834.48
06-18-07	BOUGHT 1100 SRA INTL @ 25.260	− 27791.00	25043.48
	SOLD 11 SRX SEP 25.00 CALLS @ 1.9000	+ 2074.96	27118.44
	CALLED VALUE = 27480.08 SOLD % = 6.34 EXP % = 7.46		
06-18-07	BOUGHT 1700 QLOGIC INC @ 17.030	− 28956.00	-1837.56
	SOLD 17 QLGC OCT 17.50 CALLS @ 1.2000	+ 2022.21	184.65
	CALLED VALUE = 29730.00 SOLD % = 9.65 EXP % = 6.98		
06-18-07	SOLD 3 QLGC OCT 15.00 PUTS @ .4000	+ 104.99	289.64
07-20-07	1100 GG CALLED @ 25.00	+ 27480.08	27769.72
07-23-07	BOUGHT 900 NETWORK APPLIANCE @ 31.640	− 28481.00	-711.28
	SOLD 9 NTAP SEP 32.50 CALLS @ 1.8000	+ 1604.97	893.69
	CALLED VALUE = 29230.02 SOLD % = 8.26 EXP % = 5.63		
07-23-07	SOLD 14 NTAP SEP 27.50 PUTS @ .4500	+ 614.47	1508.16
09-21-07	1100 SRX CALLED @ 25.00	+ 27480.08	28988.24
09-21-07	BUY 14 NTAP SEP 27.50 PUTS @ .6000	− 855.50	28132.74
09-21-07	SOLD 14 NTAP DEC 27.50 PUTS @ 2.4000	+ 3344.38	31477.12
09-21-07	SOLD 9 NTAP DEC 32.50 CALLS @ .5500	+ 479.98	31957.10
09-21-07	BOUGHT 1300 YHAOO INC @ 25.290	− 32882.00	-924.90
	SOLD 13 YHOO JAN 25.00 CALLS @ 2.4500	+ 3169.95	2245.05
	CALLED VALUE = 32479.91 SOLD % = 8.41 EXP % = 9.64		
10-18-07	BUY 3 QLGC OCT 15.00 PUTS @ 1.8000	− 555.00	1690.05
10-18-07	SOLD 5 QLGC JAN 15.00 PUTS @ 2.1000	+ 1034.96	2725.01
10-19-07	SOLD 17 QLGC JAN 15.00 CALLS @ .5000	+ 832.22	3557.23
12-21-07	BUY 14 NTAP DEC 27.50 PUTS @ 2.3000	− 3235.50	321.73
12-21-07	SOLD 14 NTAP MAR 27.50 PUTS @ 3.4000	+ 4744.34	5066.07
12-21-07	BUY 200 NTAP @ 25.45	− 5095.00	-28.93
12-21-07	SOLD 11 NTAP MAR 30.00 CALLS @ .7000	+ 754.97	726.04
01-18-08	BUY 5 QLGC JAN 15.00 PUTS @ 2.1500	− 1090.00	-363.96
01-18-08	SOLD 5 QLGC APR 15.00 PUTS @ 2.4500	+ 1209.96	846.00
01-18-08	SOLD 17 QLGC APR 15.00 CALLS @ .4500	+ 747.22	1593.22
01-18-08	SOLD 13 YHOO APR 25.00 CALLS @ .9500	+ 1219.95	2813.17

Scorecard # 1 *(continued)*

DATE	TRANSACTION		(+/- AMOUNT)	BALANCE
03-19-08	BUY 14 NTAP MAR 27.50 PUTS @ 8.0000	−	11215.50	-8402.33
03-19-08	SOLD 20 NTAP JUN 25.00 PUTS @ 5.8500	+	11679.61	3277.28
03-24-08	SOLD 11 NTAP JUN 27.50 CALLS @ .5000	+	534.98	3812.26
04-18-08	1300 YHOO CALLED @ 25.00	+	32479.91	36292.17
04-18-08	1700 QLGC CALLED @ 15.00	+	25480.15	61772.32
04-21-08	SOLD 10 YHOO JUL 25.00 PUTS @ 1.2000	+	1184.96	62957.28
04-21-08	BOUGHT 1200 YHAOO INC @ 28.520	−	34229.00	28728.28
	SOLD 12 YHOO JUL 27.50 CALLS @ 3.1000	+	3704.94	32433.22
	CALLED VALUE = 32979.90 SOLD % = 7.17 EXP % = 10.82			
04-21-08	BOUGHT 1500 BROADCOM @ 23.100	−	34655.00	-2221.78
	SOLD 15 BRCM AUG 22.50 CALLS @ 2.8000	+	4183.68	1961.90
	CALLED VALUE = 33729.87 SOLD % = 9.40 EXP % = 12.07			
06-20-08	BUY 2000 NTAP @ 25.00 PUT ASSIGNED	−	50019.00	-48057.10
06-24-08	SOLD 2000 NTAP @ 23.05	+	46094.74	-1962.36
06-24-08	SOLD 20 NTAP JUL 25.00 PUTS @ 2.3000	+	4579.84	2617.48
06-24-08	SOLD 11 NTAP SEP 27.50 CALLS @ .5000	+	534.98	3152.46
STOCK VALUES AT STRIKE PRICE ON EXPIRATION DATE				
07-18-08	1200 YHOO CALLED @ 27.50	+	32979.90	32979.90
08-15-08	1500 BRCM CALLED @ 22.50	+	33729.87	66709.77
09-21-08	1100 NTAP CALLED @ 27.50	+	30229.99	96939.76

```
INITIAL INVESTMENT           60000.00
STOCK VALUE AT STRIKE PRICE  96939.76
CASH IN ACCOUNT               3152.46
MARGIN INTEREST PAID              .0
TOTAL PORTFOLIO GAIN         40092.22
                                67.00  %
```

"Now I will sort for you all the trades by stock so you can see the results for each. The codes used in the stock summary are as follows:

Code after Date

P = Plan (date is in the future)
B = Buy
S = Sell
C = Called

Code at End of Transaction

CA = Call Assigned
CE = Call Expired
CO = Call Open (date is in the future)

CC = Call Closed (option was
   bought back)
PA = Put Assigned
PE = Put Expired
PO = Put Open (date is in the future)
PC = Put Closed (option was
   bought back)

< = All positions have closed (i.e. the
buy and sell cycle has completed)."

Scorecard # 1 *(continued)*

```
HISTORY BY STOCK POSITION

COMVERSE TECH                   CMVT CQV JAN APR JUL OCT
08-14-06 B     1200   19.80          23885.00  -23885.00
08-14-06 S   12 JAN   20.00   2.55    3044.95  -20840.05 CE
08-14-06 S   10 JAN   15.00    .50     484.98  -20355.07
PE
01-22-07 S   12 APR   20.00   1.25    1484.95  -18870.12 CA
04-20-07 C     1200   20.00          23980.20    5110.08 <
AVG INVESTED       23885.00       GAIN/LOSS        21.39 %


ADVANCED MICRO DEVICES          AMD  AMD JAN APR JUL OCT
01-22-07 S   10 APR   16.00    .70     684.97     684.97 PC
04-20-07 B   10 APR   16.00   1.85    1865.00   -1180.03
04-20-07 S   13 JUL   15.00   1.50    1934.92     754.89 PE


ALTERA CORP                     ALTR LTQ FEB MAY AUG NOV
08-14-06 B     1200   17.81          21377.00  -21377.00
08-14-06 S   12 DEC   17.50   1.80    2144.95  -19232.05 CA
12-15-06 C     1200   17.50          20980.30    1748.25 <
AVG INVESTED       20980.30       GAIN/LOSS         8.33 %


ROWAN COS INC                   RDC  RDC JAN APR JUL OCT
08-14-06 B      700   32.21          22552.00  -22552.00
08-14-06 S    7 OCT   32.50   2.35    1629.97  -20922.03 CE
08-14-06 S    5 OCT   30.00   1.35     659.97  -20262.06 PE
10-23-06 S    7 JAN   32.50   2.50    1734.94  -18527.12 CE
10-23-06 S    5 JAN   27.50    .85     494.98  -18032.14 PE
01-22-07 B      100   31.51          3156.00  -21188.14
01-22-07 S    8 APR   32.50   2.00    1584.94  -19603.20 CA
01-22-07 S    7 APR   27.50    .70     474.98  -19128.22 PE
04-20-07 C      800   32.50          25980.13    6851.91 <
AVG INVESTED       25708.00       GAIN/LOSS        26.65 %


TELLABS INC                     TLAB TEQ MAR JUN SEP DEC
12-18-06 B     2500   10.57          26430.00  -26430.00
12-18-06 S   25 JUN   10.00   1.60    3976.18  -22453.82 CA
06-15-07 C     2500   10.00          24980.16    2526.34 <
AVG INVESTED       24980.16       GAIN/LOSS        10.11 %
```

Scorecard # 1 *(continued)*

```
HISTORY BY STOCK POSITION

GOLD CORP                        GG  GG JAN APR JUL OCT
04-23-07 B     1100   25.65          28220.00  -28220.00
04-23-07 S   11 JUL   25.00   2.25    2459.96  -25760.04 CA
04-23-07 S    8 JUL   22.50    .45     344.98  -25415.06 PE
07-20-07 C     1100   25.00          27480.08    2065.02 <
AVG INVESTED       27480.08          GAIN/LOSS      7.51 %


SRA INTERNATIONAL               SRX SRX MAR JUN SEP DEC
04-23-07 B     1100   25.17          27692.00  -27692.00
04-23-07 S   11 JUN   25.00   1.35    1469.97  -26222.03 CA
06-15-07 C     1100   25.00          27480.08    1258.05 <
06-18-07 B     1100   25.26          27791.00  -26532.95
06-18-07 S   11 SEP   25.00   1.90    2074.96  -24457.99 CA
09-21-07 C     1100   25.00          27480.08    3022.09 <
AVG INVESTED       27480.08          GAIN/LOSS     10.99 %


NETWORK APPLIANCE               NTAP NUL MAR JUN SEP DEC
07-23-07 B      900   31.64          28481.00  -28481.00
07-23-07 S    9 SEP   32.50   1.80    1604.97  -26876.03 CE
07-23-07 S   14 SEP   27.50    .45     614.47  -26261.56 PC
09-21-07 B   14 SEP   27.50    .60     885.50  -27147.06
09-21-07 S   14 DEC   27.50   2.40    3344.38  -23802.68 PC
09-21-07 S    9 DEC   32.50    .55     479.98  -23322.70 CE
12-21-07 B   14 DEC   27.50   2.30    3235.50  -26558.20
12-21-07 S   14 MAR   27.50   3.40    4744.34  -21813.86 PC
12-21-07 B      200   25.45          5095.00  -26908.86
12-21-07 S   11 MAR   30.00    .70     754.97  -26153.89 CE
03-20-08 B   14 MAR   27.50   8.00   11215.50  -37369.39
03-20-08 S   20 JUN   25.00   5.85   11679.61  -25689.78 PA
03-24-08 S   11 JUN   27.50    .50     534.98  -25154.80 CE
06-20-08 B     2000   25.00          50019.00  -75173.80
06-24-08 S     2000   22.99          46094.74  -29079.06 <
06-24-08 S   20 JUL   25.00   2.30    4579.84  -24499.22 PO
06-24-08 S   11 SEP   27.50    .50     534.98  -23964.24 CO
09-19-08 P     1100   27.50          30229.99    6265.75 <
AVG INVESTED       33571.00          GAIN/LOSS     18.66 %
```

Scorecard # 1 *(continued)*

```
HISTORY BY STOCK POSITION

YAHOO INC                      YHOO YHQ JAN APR JUL OCT
09-21-07 B     1300  25.29          32882.00  -32882.00
09-21-07 S    13 JAN  25.00   2.45   3169.95  -29712.05 CE
01-18-08 S    13 APR  25.00    .95   1219.95  -28492.10 CA
04-18-08 C     1300  25.00          32479.91   3987.81 <
AVG INVESTED       32479.91   GAIN/LOSS          12.27 %

04-21-08 B     1200  28.52          34229.00  -34229.00
04-21-08 S    12 JUL  27.50   3.10   3704.94  -30524.06 CO
04-21-08 S    10 JUL  25.00   1.20   1184.96  -29339.10 PO
07-18-08 P     1200  27.50          32979.90   3640.80 <
AVG INVESTED       32979.90   GAIN/LOSS          11.03 %

BROADCOM                       BRCM RCQ FEB MAY AUG NOV
04-21-08 B     1500  23.10          34655.00  -34655.00
04-21-08 S    15 AUG  22.50   2.80   4183.68  -30471.32 CO
08-15-08 P     1500  22.50          33729.87   3258.55 <
AVG INVESTED       33729.87   GAIN/LOSS           9.66 %

QLOGIC CORP                    QLGC QLQ JAN APR JUL OCT
06-18-07 B     1700  17.03          28956.00  -28956.00
06-18-07 S    17 OCT  17.50   1.20   2022.21  -26933.79 CE
06-18-07 S     3 OCT  15.00    .40    104.99  -26828.80 PC
10-18-07 B     3 OCT  15.00   1.80    555.00  -27383.80
10-18-07 S     5 JAN  15.00   2.10   1034.96  -26348.84 PC
10-19-07 S    17 JAN  15.00    .50    832.22  -25516.62 CE
01-18-08 B     5 JAN  15.00   2.15   1090.00  -26606.62
01-18-08 S     5 APR  15.00   2.45   1209.96  -25396.66 PE
01-18-08 S    17 APR  15.00    .45    747.22  -24649.44 CA
04-18-08 C     1700  15.00          25480.15    830.71 <
AVG INVESTED       28956.00   GAIN/LOSS           2.86 %
```

Again, there was a round of applause. It appeared that investors certainly felt they had gotten their money's worth.

Steve Malcolm came to center stage. "Professor Graham, this has been a very illuminating presentation. I would like to ask one final question. Are you a bull or a bear with respect to the next few years?"

Professor Graham smiled. This was a question he could always expect. "I recently came across a chart that this group might find interesting. It's called 'Historical Buy & Sell Time Line' and goes from the year 1850 to 2018. I've been referring to it as the Cedric Chart because I learned about it from a newspaper column by Cedric Adams, a famous

Cedric Chart

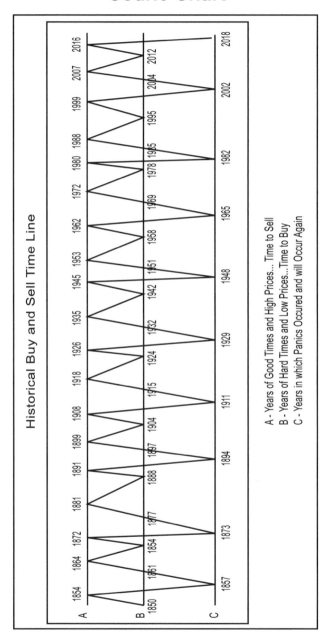

Historical Buy and Sell Time Line

A - Years of Good Times and High Prices... Time to Sell
B - Years of Hard Times and Low Prices....Time to Buy
C - Years in which Panics Occured and will Occur Again

Minnesota newspaper columnist and radio personality very popular in the 1950s. Let's see if I can pull it up and flash it on the screens.

"Ah, here we go. I will leave it to you to decide the predictive value of the chart. I have personally been impressed with how 'right on' the chart has been in prior years. If it is accurate we will experience a downswing until 2012. My strategy will emphasize ITM Covered Calls until then. Beginning around 2012 we should have a six-year bull market. Then look out for a big drop going into 2018."

Steve Malcolm continued to stare at the Cedric Chart. Finally he looked at the Professor and said, "Thanks Professor for the wonderful insights into taking investment matters into our own hands. Perhaps I can get you to visit me on my TV show. If anyone else has a question for the professor and does not get it answered before the end of the cruise, he has agreed to accept questions at robgrahamphd@aol.com."

Later that evening, Jake and Katie invited Rob and Jean Graham to join them on the balcony of their stateroom. Katie brought out mugs of decaf as they enjoyed the view of the full moon glistening on the Caribbean and reflected on the events of the past year.

Jake noticed that Katie and Jean were engrossed in their own conversation. As he tasted the coffee he noticed a meteor cross the sky. Finally, Jake broached a subject that had been on his mind lately. "Professor, I wonder if we are doing the right thing by sharing your money tree strategy with the whole world. Maybe we should just keep it to ourselves?"

Rob smiled at Jake. *Ah, still the student.* "Jake, did you notice how excited the audience was tonight. They seemed ready to reach for a higher level of investing maturity. I wouldn't trade that experience for all the gold in Ft. Knox."

They were quiet for a few moments. Then Rob turned to Jake and said, "In fact, I think you and I should write that book."

Glossary

American Stock Exchange (AMEX)—a private, not-for-profit corporation, located in New York City, that handles approximately one-fifth of all securities trades within the United States.

American Style Option—an option contract that can be exercised at any time between the date of purchase and the expiration date. The other type of contract is the European Style which may be exercised only during a specified period of time just prior to its expiration. Most exchange-traded options are American style.

Arbitrage—the simultaneous purchase and sale of identical financial instruments in order to make a profit where the selling price is higher than the buying price.

Arbitrageur—an individual that takes advantage of momentary disparities in prices between markets which enables one to lock in profits because the selling price is higher than the buying price.

Ask Price—the current cost to buy a security or option. It is the lowest price the seller will accept at that time.

At-The-Money (ATM)—when an option's strike price is the same as the price of the underlying stock.

Automatic Exercise—the automatic exercise of an option that is in-the-money on expiration date.

Bare Cash—a company's cash plus marketable securities less long term debt.

Bear—an investor whose sentiment or belief is that a security or the market is falling or is expected to fall.

Bear Call Spread—a strategy in which a trader sells a lower strike call and buys a higher strike call to create a trade with limited profit and limited risk. A fall in the price of the underlying stock increases the value of the spread. This is a net credit (cash inflow) transaction. The maximum loss is the difference between the strike prices less the credit. The maximum gain equals the credit.

Bear Market—the stock market cycle where prices for the overall market fall for an extended period of time, usually caused by a weak economy and subsequent decreased corporate profits. It is generally agreed that a bear market is when the stock market experiences a price decline of twenty percent or more, and lasts at least two months.

Bear Put Spread—a strategy in which a trader sells a lower strike put and buys a higher strike put to create a trade with limited profit and limited risk. A fall in the price of the underlying stock increases the value of the spread. This is a net debit (cash outflow) transaction. The maximum gain is the difference between the strike prices less the debit. The maximum loss is equal to the debit.

Bid Price—the current price you would receive if a stock (or option) is sold. It is the highest price the buyer will pay for that security at the present time.

Black Scholes Formula—a pricing model that is used by most options exchanges to price various options. It factors in the current stock price, strike price, time until expiration, current interest rates, and volatility of the underlying security.

Break-even—the price of an underlying security at which an option strategy neither gains nor loses money.

Bull—an investor whose sentiment or belief is that a security or the market is rising or is expected to rise.

Bull Market—the stock market cycle where prices for the overall market rise for an extended period of time usually caused by a strong economy and subsequent increased corporate profits.

Bull Call Spread—a strategy in which a trader buys a lower strike call and sells a higher strike call to create a trade with limited profit and limited risk. A rise in the price of the underlying stock increases the value of the spread. This is a net debit (cash outflow) transaction. The maximum loss is equal to the initial debit. The maximum gain is the difference between the strike prices less the debit.

Bull Put Spread—a strategy in which a trader sells a higher strike put and buys a lower strike put to create a trade with limited profit and limited risk. A rise in the price of the underlying stock increases the value of the spread. This is a net credit (cash inflow) transaction. The maximum loss is the difference between the strike prices less credit. The maximum gain is equal to the credit.

Buy Limit—the maximum price that should ever be paid for a stock, based on its 52 week low (L) and 52 week high (H).

$$\text{Buy Limit} = L + .25 \times (H - L)$$

Buy Rank—a formula to rank the relative appeal of stocks on the prospect list. In the formula BL is Buy Limit, CP is current price, H is the 52 week high and L is the 52 week low.

$$\text{Buy Rank} = \frac{10 \times (BL - CP)}{.25 \times (H - L)}$$

Call Option—a contract that gives the holder the right (but not the obligation) to buy a specific stock at a predetermined price on or before a certain date (called the expiration date).

Chicago Board Options Exchange (CBOE)—the largest options exchange in the United States.

Covered Call—a short call option position against a long position in the underlying stock or index.

Covered Put—a short put option position against a short position in the underlying stock or index.

Double Up—a strategy where one executes both a covered call and naked put with the same expiration date.

Earnings—A company's revenues minus cost of sales, operating expenses, and taxes, over a given period of time.

European Style Option—an option contract that may be exercised only during a specified period of time just prior to its expiration.

Exercise—implementing an option owner's right to buy or sell the underlying security.

Exercise Price—see strike price.

Expiration—the date and time after which an option may no longer be exercised.

Expiration Date—the last day on which an option may be exercised.

Fundamental Analysis—evaluating a company to determine if it is a good investment risk. Evaluation is based mainly on balance sheet and income statements, past records of earnings, sales, assets, management, products and services.

Go Long—to buy securities or options.

Gold $—a chart calculation that indicates when to take action and invest in the stock being watched. It is 10 x number of up days, plus 2 x number of days in the VISIONS View V, plus 30 if currently trading in the V or within 5% of the 50 day moving average. A value of 100 is ideal.

Good 'Till Canceled Order (GTC)—Sometimes simply called *GTC* it means an order to buy or sell stock that is good until you cancel it.

Go Short—to sell securities or options.

Holder—one who purchases an option.

Index—an index is a group of stocks which can be traded as one portfolio, such as the S&P 500. Broad-based indexes cover a wide range of industries and companies and narrow-based indexes cover stocks in one industry or economic sector.

Index Options—call and put options on indexes of stocks that allow investors to trade in a specific industry group or market without having to buy all the stocks individually.

In-the-Money (ITM)—an option is In-the-Money to the extent it has intrinsic value. (See Intrinsic Value). A call option is said to be In-the-Money when the price of the underlying stock is higher than the strike price of the option. A put option is said to be In-the-Money when the price of the underlying stock is lower than the strike price of the option.

Intrinsic Value—a call option premium is said to have intrinsic value to the extent the stock price exceeds the strike price. A put option premium is said to have intrinsic value to the extent the strike price exceeds the stock price. The total value of the premium is intrinsic value (if any) plus the time value.

LEAPS (Long-term Equity AnticiPation Securities)—long dated options with expiration dates up to three years in the future.

Limit Order—a condition on a transaction to buy at or below a specified price or to sell at or above a specified price.

Long—a long position indicates that a stock, index, or option is owned.

Margin—a loan by a broker to allow an investor to buy more stocks or options than available money (cash) in the account.

Margin Requirements (Options)—the amount of cash an uncovered (naked) option writer is required to deposit and maintain to cover his daily position price changes.

Market Cap—This is a company's market capitalization which equals the number of outstanding shares times the current market price.

Market Order—an order that is filled immediately upon reaching the trading floor at the next best available price.

Naked Call—a short call option in which the writer does not own the underlying security. Same as Uncovered Call.

Naked Put—a short put option in which the writer does not have a corresponding short position on the underlying security. Same as Uncovered Put.

NASDAQ (National Association of Securities Dealers Automated Quotations)—a computerized system providing brokers and dealers with price quotations for securities traded over-the-counter as well as for many New York Stock Exchange listed securities.

New York Stock Exchange (NYSE)—the largest stock exchange in the United States.

Option—a security that represents the right, but not the obligation, to buy or sell a specified amount of an underlying security (stock, bond, futures contract, etc.) at a specified price within a specified time.

Option Class—a group of calls or a group of puts on the same stock.

Option Holder—the buyer of either a call or put option.

Option Premium—the price it paid to buy an option or the price received for selling an option.

Option Series—call or put options in the same class that have the same expiration date and strike price.

Option Writer—the seller of either a call or put option.

Out-of-the-Money—an option whose exercise price has no intrinsic value.

Out-of-the-Money Option (OTM)—a call option is out-of-the-money if its exercise or strike price is above the current market price of the underlying security. A put option is out-of-the-money if its exercise or strike price is below the current market price of the underlying security.

Portfolio Income Explorer—a software program that searches for the best call options for any list of stocks at any time.

Premium—see Option Premium.

Price to Earnings Ratio (PE)—the current stock price divided by the earnings per share for the past year.

Put Factor—A formula to guide the selection of a naked put strike price and strike month. A factor greater than one is desirable. In the formula, PR is the naked put premium, SP is the strike price, CP is the current stock price, and ME is months to expiration.

$$\text{Put Factor} = \frac{6\ (100\ PR)\ (CP\text{-}SP)}{(ME)\ (SP)\ (SP)}$$

Put Option—a contract that gives the right (but not the obligation) to sell a specific stock at a predetermined price on or before a certain date (called the expiration date).

Revenue—The amount of money a company brought in during the time period covered by the income statement. This is usually the first line on any income statement and is also sometimes referred to as total sales.

Ride the Wave—a strategy where one sells Covered Calls and Naked Puts on the same stock over and over as the stock trades in a wave like pattern.

Sales—The amount of money a company brought in during the time period covered by the income statement. This is usually the first line on any income statement and is also sometimes referred to as total revenue.

Security—a trading instrument such as stocks, bonds, and short-term investments.

Short—a short position indicates that a stock, index, or option is not owned.

Spread—the price gap between the bid and ask price of a stock.

Stock—a share of a company's stock translates into ownership of part of the company.

Stock Split—an increase in the number of stock shares with a corresponding decrease in the par value of a company's stock.

Straddle—a position consisting of a long call and a long put, or a short call and a short put, where both options have the same underlying security, strike price and expiration date.

Strangle—a position consisting of a long call and a long put or a short call and a short put, where both options have the same underlying security, the same expiration date, but different strike prices.

Strike Price—also called the exercise price, is the price at which a call option holder can purchase the underlying stock by exercising the option, and is the price at which a put option holder can sell the underlying stock by exercising the option.

TAI—Take Action Indicator. Formula for determining the relative attractiveness of stocks on the prospect list. In the formula BR is Buy Rank, FDA is Fifty Day Moving Average and CP is the current stock price.

$$TAI = BR \times \left(1 + \frac{FDA}{2 \times (FDA) - CP} \right)$$

Technical Analysis—a method of evaluating securities and options by analyzing statistics generated by market activity, such as past high/low, up/down volume, momentum and moving averages.

Time Value—an option's premium consists of two parts: time value and intrinsic value. (See Intrinsic Value) The time value portion of the premium deteriorates with the passage of time and becomes zero with the expiration of the option.

Triple Witching Day—the third Friday in March, June, September and December when U.S. options, future options, and index options all expire on the same day.

Uncovered Call—a short call option in which the writer does not own the underlying security.

Uncovered Put—a short put option in which the writer does not have a corresponding short position on the underlying security.

VISIONS Portfolio Income Explorer—a Personal Internet Search Engine that can find the best call options for any list of stocks. It returns the best near term call option and calculates the potential monthly and yearly income.

VISIONS Stock Explorer—a Personal Internet Search Engine that gets the fundamental data on any stock and provides all the technical indicators on a VISIONS stock chart.

VISIONS Stock Market Explorer—a full featured Personal Internet Search Engine that can find the best stocks and call or put options that meet various search criteria. It provides tools for information filtering and sorting. It provides stock charts, which include the Buy Limit, 50-Day Average, Buy Rank, the VISIONS View V, and take action indicators.

VISIONS View V—an indicator on a VISIONS chart that shows when it is time to take action and invest in a particular stock.

Web Site—An information location on the Internet. Each web site has a unique address called a URL that one uses to access the site and obtain information or transact business. The URL to download the VISIONS software is www.RonGroenke.com. The URL for Keller Publishing is www.KellerPublishing.com.

Writer—the seller of an option.

Appendix A
Placing the Trade

When placing option trading orders it is very important to state exactly what is intended. If a mistake is made and you execute a wrong trade you may incur a loss to undo it.

Option orders like stock orders can be placed in your brokerage account over the phone by calling a trader, over the phone with direct keypad input, or over the Internet with on line access to your account. No matter which way you trade, the way an order is placed is important.

Here are some key terms you should know.

Sell to Open—You are opening a short position for a specific option. This is what you use to write a covered call.

Buy to Close—You are buying back an option you previously sold, to close out the option. This is what you would do if you did not want your stock to be called. Also, you would want to do this if you want to sell the stock. Selling the stock without buying back the call option would leave you in a high-risk, uncovered position.

Buy to Open—You are opening a long position for a specific option. This is what you do when you are taking a leveraged position by buying the option instead of the stock.

Sell to Close—You are closing a long position for a specific option. This is what you do to capture a gain on your leveraged position.

Market order—The order will be executed at the next available bid price. Use this to buy or sell immediately.

Limit order—The order is executed at the limit price or better if possible.

For the day—The order called a Day order will expire at the end of the trading day.

All or none (AON)—Buy or sell the number of contracts specified. This condition is used to reduce the possibility of trading only one or a small number of contracts in a multiple contract order. Additional orders may increase your overall commission cost.

Good till canceled (GTC)—The order is open until it is canceled. Most brokerage firms will close GTC orders after ninety days.

Appendix B
Record Keeping

When your order is filled, write out the detail of the order and the net proceeds of the action on your daily-completed order sheet. Save these sheets until you receive your confirmation from your broker. This is a precautionary measure only. If there are errors in the confirmation you need documentation to perform resolution. You will also need your daily trade results sheet to update your trading files and track your overall results.

After I started trading options it became important to record and track each and every trade. I have done this since day one and now have the history of every trade I made in my blue file. Why a blue file? For every trade you execute you will receive a trade confirmation in the mail from your broker. To keep these together and easily accessible I put them in a blue file folder instead of the standard cream colored ones. This allowed me to find this file very quickly since I was using it more and more each day. I also have a box on the daily order sheets, which gets checked indicating that the blue file was updated.

In this blue file folder I have a transaction history tracking sheet on which I record my daily transactions such as, stock buys, call option sales, assignments, close outs, etc. I record the date, the transaction, and the net debit or credit for the trade. This is a running list and fills multiple pages for the year. After receiving the confirmation from the broker I use a highlighter and highlight the debit or credit on the tracking sheet to indicate that I received the trade confirmation and the results agree. The confirmations are filed in the order of the tracking sheet. This allows quick access if a reference is required. If a transaction is not highlighted within two weeks, I call the brokerage house and ask for a duplicate confirmation. It may not have been sent or it may have gotten lost in the mail. This process makes sure there is a paper trail for every transaction for tax or other purposes such as stockholder class action lawsuits. In the latter situation, you may be asked to provide copies of all transactions during a certain period to substantiate a possible claim and participate in any settlement. My greatest use of this record was the settlement on litigation regarding the NASDAQ market makers spread price fixing antitrust action. This was an instance where the U.S. Department of Justice brought a civil enforcement proceeding on July 17, 1996, alleging that twenty-four NASDAQ market makers, together with others, conspired to widen spreads in violation of the federal antitrust laws. To participate in this settlement, one had to supply detail records of related NASDAQ stock transactions for the defined period.

The blue file contains all transactions in the order of execution by date. I also maintain a group of computer files called directory nineteen. In this directory I maintain a file by company of every transaction executed. From this directory I can extract every trade on any company that I have invested in and print out the trading history and corresponding overall gain or loss. I process this directory on a periodic basis to update my successful company list and to track overall results. I use the stock symbol as the file name, which prevents duplication while still being very informative. I backup this directory monthly and keep multiple backups for history and recovery if needed. All of the examples in this book are from this history file."

One other important record-keeping requirement is a tax file. For taxes, you need to actually move some cash from your brokerage account to a savings or money market account. This way you are not tempted to invest it. It is reserved for taxes so leave it there. You do not want to have to close out some calls and sell some stock to make your quarterly tax payments. It could be bad timing. Remember we are reserving for taxes because we plan to make money. It is one of the perks when you have gains. The amount to reserve depends on your tax bracket, but here is good formula:

$$\text{Tax Reserve} = .25 \times (\text{Total Option Premiums} - \text{Losses})$$

146

Appendix C
Investing Tools

Now that you have gained the knowledge of the *Show Me the Money* concepts, your profits will be greatly enhanced by specially designed software programs reviewed on the pages that follow.

The screen shots provided here are just a sampling of the power of the VISIONS Stock Market Explorer, the Portfolio Income Explorer, Stock Explorer, EZ Link, the Money Tree Tools, and the Stock Market Simulator.

You can experience this software free of charge by downloading and running a trial copy from my web site **www.Ron Groenke.com**

VISIONS Stock Market Explorer: A Stock and Options Search Engine—
This dynamic program eliminates the drudgery of looking for the
financial information for the companies that you might want to analyze and add to your prospect list. The major functions are shown on
the Home Page. Each button below activates the function as named,
which are further described below.

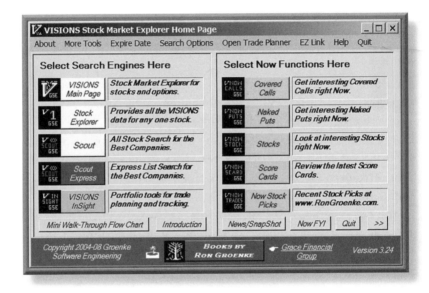

VISIONS Scout: An Automated Full Stock Market Search Engine—With the touch of one button this search engine will search the entire stock market and return a list of the Top Ten companies that meet the ideal stock selection criteria as outlined in this book. This includes the fundamental financial analysis and the technical chart analysis.

Financial analysis looks at Market Cap, Revenue Growth, Quarterly Earnings, Revenue/Sales, Bare Cash, Volume of shares traded per day and Buy Rank. The technical chart analysis looks at where each stock is trading in relation to the VISIONS View V, Take Action status, and its Gold $ Score. Stocks that pass all the Ideal Criteria are candidates for the Top Ten list. The Scout Report shows the detail data for all the stocks passing the technical criteria and are shown in order with the Top Ten at front of the list.

There is nothing like Scout available in the financial community. It is unique and gives you the control to find the best investment opportunities right now any day any time.

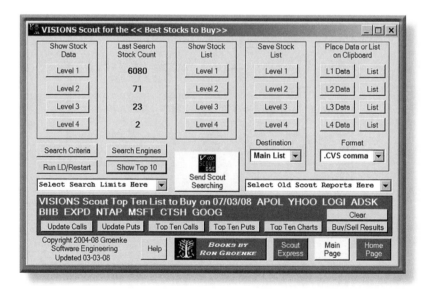

VISIONS Scout Search Report

Print Find Calendar Throw Away Export Data Export Data to Clipboard 23 Entries Split Report

Scout Stocks to Buy Report 07/03/08 12:12PM

Scout Stocks to Buy Report 07/03/08 10:12PM

Results after Searching the NASDAQ 100

Company Name	Stock Symbol	Search Date	Quote	# Up Days	#Days In V Score	Gold$ Score	52Wk High	52Wk Low	50Day Avg	Buy Limit	Buy Rank	TA I @ TAI	#Days Best Fit	Beta	P/E	Div Yld%	Opn ?	Vol/ Day	Mkt Cap	Bare Cash	Rev/ Year	% Rev Gth/Y	Qtryl Erngs
APOLLO GP INC	APOL	07-08-08	55.18	0	30	100	81.68	37.92	48.36	48.86	-5.78	BI	2	*	0.62	27.6	0	Y	4M	9B	31M	2B	14.9	+++
YAHOO INC	YHOO	07-08-08	21.35	2	10	70	34.08	18.58	24.79	22.45	2.83	TA	2	**	0.87	28.9	0	Y	41M	29B	487M	7B	8.7	++++
LOGITECH INT S	LOGI	07-08-08	25.73	1	10	60	37.23	23.39	30.09	26.85	3.23	TA	10	***	2.41	20.9	0	Y	1M	4B	3M	2B	17.3	++++
AUTODESK INC	ADSK	07-08-08	33.96	1	9	58	51.32	29.58	38.51	35.01	1.93	TA	9	***	2.10	22.1	0	Y	3M	7B	31M	2B	17.7	++++
BIOGEN IDEC IN	BIIB	07-08-08	58.20	0	14	58	84.75	53.50	60.38	61.31	3.98	TA	3	***	0.76	26.9	0	Y	2M	17B	472M	3B	31.6	++++
EXPEDITORS INT	EXPD	07-08-08	21.81	1	6	52	54.46	38.16	44.90	42.23	1.03	TA	3	***	0.71	33.5	0.7	Y	1M	8B	670K	5B	16.8	++++
NETAPP INC	NTAP	07-08-08	21.94	0	10	20	32.84	19.00	23.92	22.46	1.50	TA	10	***	1.51	25.6	0	Y	8M	7B	55M	3B	17.0	++++
MICROSOFT CP	MSFT	07-08-08	25.98	1	18	46	37.50	23.19	28.17	26.76	2.18	TA	6	***	1.27	15.1	1.6	Y	69M	241B	17B	57B	0.4	++++
COGNIZANT TECH	CTSH	07-08-08	21.89	1	2	46	44.44	23.37	33.53	28.63	-6.02	BI	3	*	1.43	25.5	0	Y	4M	9B	330M	2B	39.7	++++
GOOGLE	GOOG	07-08-08	537.00	0	44	44	747.24	412.11	558.89	495.89	-4.91	WT	6	***	2.16	37.1	0	Y	5M	168B	8B	18B	41.5	++++
GARMIN LTD	GRMN	07-08-08	41.95	0	21	40	125.68	39.75	46.30	61.23	8.97	GR	20	***	1.29	10.7	1.8	Y	4M	9B	37M	3B	34.9	++++
INTEL CP	INTC	07-08-08	20.66	0	5	40	27.99	18.05	22.88	20.53	-0.53	TA	2	***	1.41	18.1	2.6	Y	55M	109B	3B	39B	9.3	++++
PAYCHEX INC	PAYX	07-08-08	21.04	1	13	36	47.14	30.09	33.58	34.35	7.76	GR	9	***	0.99	19.9	3.8	Y	3M	11B	511M	2B	6.5	++++
AKAMAI TECH IN	AKAM	07-08-08	32.97	0	36	36	50.98	25.06	36.86	31.54	-2.21	TA	1	***	1.88	50.4	0	Y	4M	5B	201M	684B	34.3	++++
C.H. ROBINSON	CHRW	07-08-08	52.37	0	2	34	67.36	45.01	60.65	50.59	-3.19	WT	2	***	1.27	27.0	1.6	Y	1M	8B	115M	7B	22.6	++++
EBAY INC	EBAY	07-08-08	26.80	0	16	32	40.73	25.10	29.12	29.00	5.63	GR	2	***	1.69	85.1	0	Y	14M	35B	658M	8B	24.0	++-
JUNIPER NETWOR	JNPR	07-08-08	22.75	2	5	30	37.95	21.38	25.42	25.52	6.68	GR	15	***	1.69	32.0	0	Y	12M	11B	240M	3B	31.3	++++
BROADCOM CROP	BRCM	07-08-08	26.22	0	0	30	43.07	16.38	26.95	23.05	-4.76	WT	11	***	2.34	65.6	0	Y	14M	13B	141M	3B	14.5	++++
CISCO SYS INC	CSCO	07-08-08	23.12	1	8	26	34.24	21.77	25.46	24.88	5.64	GR	6	***	1.49	18.1	0	Y	50M	136B	12B	38B	10.4	++++
MONSTER WORLDW	MNST	07-08-08	18.41	0	12	24	43.29	18.23	23.14	24.99	9.70	GR	29	****	1.82	18.3	0	Y	2M	2B	448M	1B	12.6	++++
NVIDIA CORP	NVDA	07-08-08	12.49	0	11	22	39.67	12.40	21.70	19.21	9.85	GR	12	****	2.65	9.0	0	Y	22M	6B	1B	4B	36.6	++++
CITRIX SYSTEMS	CTXS	07-08-08	28.59	0	7	14	43.90	28.31	32.92	32.30	9.26	GR	6	***	1.33	25.6	0	Y	3M	5B	356M	1B	22.4	++++
FOCUS MEDIA HO	FMCN	07-08-08	26.98	0	3	6	66.30	26.15	33.14	36.18	9.16	GR	19	***	3.14	46.0	0	Y	4M	3B	90M	616M	214.7	-+++

THE STOCK SEARCH ENGINE—A data-mining machine that gets the data on any list of companies and finds the diamonds (companies with the highest best fit ranking) for investment consideration. It allows you to filter and sort the list to your specified criteria such as Buy Rank, Yearly Revenue Growth, Dividend Yield, PE, Trading Volume, Market Cap, Bare Cash, and many more. Searches can be performed on the supplied lists or on those you create and save.

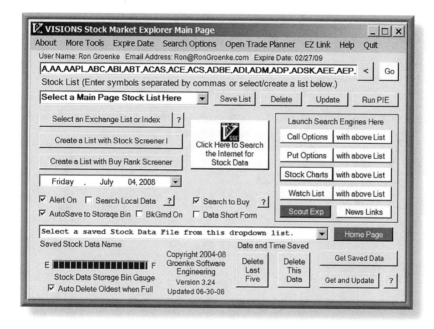

Stock Search Results with filter panel

From your VISIONS Storage Bin, AutoSave Results for List [SRCE,TW,COMS,01-19-06 02-30 PM

Print New Report Save Data Save Symbols Throw Away Set/Show Filters UnDo Sort Help Best Fit Key Help/Definitions Web Links BL/BR Wizard Data is Filtered

Company Name	Stock Symbol	Search Date	Quote	52Wk High	52Wk Low	50Day Avg	Buy Limit	Buy Rank I	TA	Best Fit Beta	P/E	Div Ylds	Opn ?	Vol/ Day	Mkt Cap	Bare Cash	Rev/ Cash Year	% Rev Gth/Yr	Qtrly Erngs
VERISIGN INC	VRSN	01-19-06	22.30	33.36	19.01	22.24	22.59	0.800	TA ****	3.49	23.8	0	Y	4M	5B	737M	1B	27.5	++++
W HOLDING CO I	WHI	01-19-06	8.94	14.18	7.31	8.45	9.02	0.46	TA ***	0.54	10.4	2.2	N	524K	1B	973M	329M	10.6	--+
PLANTRONICS IN	PLT	01-19-06	30.36	41.01	26.40	29.27	30.05	-0.85	TA ***	2.09	17.7	0.6	Y	538K	1B	242M	619M	32.3	++++
PACIFIC SUNWEA	PSUN	01-19-06	23.03	29.05	20.33	24.56	22.51	-2.39	TA ***	1.22	14.6	0	Y	1M	1B	143M	1B	13.6	+--
P.F.CHANG'S C	PFCB	01-19-06	47.28	65.12	42.92	50.69	48.47	2.14	TA ***	0.86	32.9	0	Y	570K	1B	70M	794M	16.7	++++
MITTAL STEEL C	MT	01-19-06	27.92	43.86	22.11	27.21	27.54	-0.70	TA ***	1.51	4.4	1.4	Y	1M	19B	2B	27B	12.0	-++
LIFEPOINT HOSP	LPNT	01-19-06	31.89	51.54	28.57	36.42	34.31	4.21	TA ***	0.00	20.7	0	Y	1M	1B	18M	3B	117.7	++++
KINDRED HEALTH	KND	01-19-06	28.33	42.11	24.74	26.83	29.98	1.72	TA ***	0.33	9.2	0	Y	510K	1B	281M	3B	10.7	++++
INVITROGEN COR	IVGN	01-19-06	68.97	88.50	60.14	67.48	67.23	-2.46	TA ***	0.63	33.9	0	Y	1M	3B	967M	1B	13.0	++++
HLTH MGMT ASSO	HMA	01-19-06	22.32	27.00	20.75	22.64	22.31	-0.07	TA ***	0.00	15.8	1.1	Y	1M	5B	89M	3B	10.8	++++
COOPER COS INC	COO	01-19-06	52.72	84.70	44.75	51.47	54.73	2.01	TA ***	0.00	26.4	0.1	Y	1M	2B	8M	807M	69.3	++++
CAREER EDUCATI	CECO	01-19-06	21.14	41.75	28.73	33.69	31.98	2.58	TA ***	0.11	14.4	0	Y	1M	3B	331M	2B	14.1	++++
CABELAS INC	CAB	01-19-06	16.38	23.25	15.34	17.24	17.31	4.70	TA ***	0.86	15.9	0	Y	397K	1B	85M	1B	12.0	++++
BED BATH & BEY	BBY	01-19-06	37.10	46.99	34.85	38.38	37.88	2.57	TA ***	0.98	20.1	0	Y	3M	11B	851M	5B	11.0	++++
AMER PHARMA PT	APPX	01-19-06	37.76	58.73	32.25	38.22	38.86	1.66	TA ***	0.45	32.9	0	Y	717K	2B	67M	496M	34.7	++++

Visions Stock Filters

A | B | C | D | E | F   X

Set these filters to the criteria for your search.

Stock Symbols	Stock Price	P/E Ratio	Buy Rank (1)	TAI (1)	Best Fit (1)	Beta	Share Vol/Day	Options Req'd	Market Cap	Rev/Year	Rev Grown/Yr	Bare Cash	Qtrly Earnings
Any	Any	Any	Any	=TA	>blank	Any	Any	Any	> 500M	>250M	> 10%	Any	All 4 of 4 +

Get A Set   Do UnDo Set All to Any

Select Favorite then Get to retrieve filter template.

Select Favorite, enter name, then set to save template.

Copyright 2004 Groenke Software Engineering

THE STOCK CHART SEARCH ENGINE—Displays a 12 month view of the stocks on your list together with their Buy Limit, 30, 50, 100, or 200 day moving average, and comparison with the major indexes such as the DJIA, SP500, SP100, NASDAQ, or Russell 2000. Provides a take action indicator with number of days in the VISIONS View V. Charts are saved for use at any time.

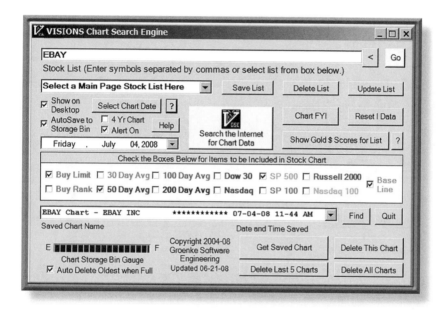

Standard Chart

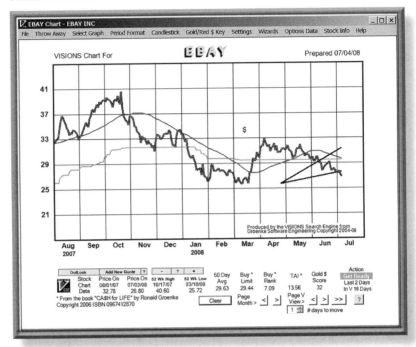

Candlestick view

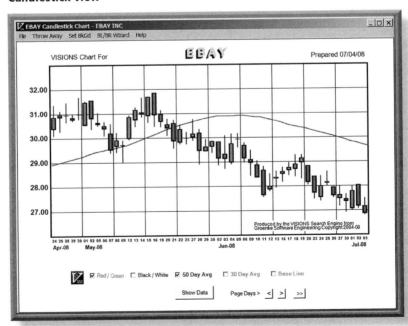

THE CALL OPTION SEARCH ENGINE—Displays the call options that meet your strike month, % gain, and premium criteria. It also provides the current price, the 52-week trading range, 50-day average, Buy Limit, Buy Rank, TAI, and Beta. A best fit to the Magic Chart is calculated along with percent gain for If-Sold and If-Expired, and months to expiration. Creates a summary of all the options sorted by best If-Sold % gain from all the stocks in your search list.

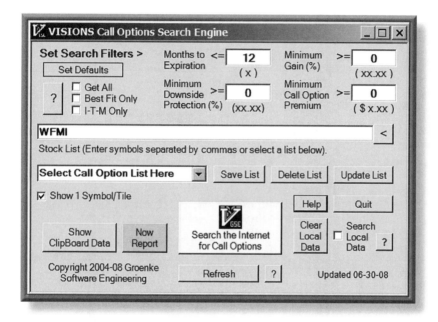

Sample Call Options for one Stock WFMI

Call Options for WHOLE FOODS MARKT [WFMI] On 12/10/07 10:11 AM price < 50DayAvg TAI=Bad Idea

Print Throw Away Change Stock Price to My Purchase Price Export Data Get Chart

Call Options for WHOLE FOODS MARKET [WFMI] On 12/10/07 10:11 AM Price < 50DayAvg TAI=Bad Idea
Price 43.00 (-0.05) 52WkHi 53.65 53WkLow 36.00 50DayAvg 42.25 BuyLimit 40.41 BuyRank -5.87 Beta 1.15

Option Symbol	Strike Date	Strike Price	Call Option Premium Bid	Asked	Open Interest	% Gain If Sold	% Gain If Exprd	*Magic Chart* % If Sold	% If Exprd	Mths Till Exp	Best Fit	Break Even Price	Down Side (%)	Bid/ StkPr (%)
FMQLH	12/21/07	40.00	3.15	3.25	1,655	0.35	7.33	2.72	2.16	<1	*	39.85	7.33	7.88
FMQLI	12/21/07	45.00	0.36	0.39	4,921	5.49	0.84	2.72	2.16	<1	*	42.64	0.84	0.80
FMQAH	1/18/07	35.00	8.05	8.20	1,747	0.12	18.72	6.80	5.40	1		34.95	18.72	23.00
FMQAH	1/18/07	40.00	3.75	3.90	3,725	1.74	8.72	6.80	5.40	1	*	39.25	8.72	9.38
FMQAB	1/18/07	42.50	2.17	2.22	4,519	3.88	5.05	6.80	5.40	1	*	40.83	5.05	5.11
FMQAI	1/18/07	45.00	1.06	1.10	7,012	7.12	2.47	6.80	5.40	1	*	41.94	2.47	2.36
FMQAC	1/18/07	47.50	0.47	0.50	4,115	11.56	1.09	6.80	5.40	1	*	42.53	1.09	0.99
FMQAJ	1/18/07	50.00	0.20	0.22	9,866	16.74	0.47	6.80	5.40	1	*	42.80	0.47	0.40
FMQBG	2/15/08	35.00	8.40	8.50	977	0.93	19.53	8.40	6.70	2	*	34.60	19.53	24.00
FMQBH	2/15/08	40.00	4.45	4.60	2,533	3.37	10.35	8.40	6.70	2	*	38.55	10.35	11.13
FMQBI	2/15/08	45.00	1.85	1.90	2,928	8.95	4.30	8.40	6.70	2	*	41.15	4.30	4.11
FMQBJ	2/15/08	50.00	0.60	0.63	2,833	17.67	1.40	8.40	6.70	2	*	42.40	1.40	1.20

Call Options filtered and sorted for a list of stocks

Call Options For [INTC,SNDK,GE,BSC,IMCL,] — 12-10-07 10:25 AM

Edit Print Data>Clipbd UnDo Show Stk Data Show Bar Graph Sort If Sold Sort If Exprd Sort by Date Filter Throw Away Get/Save Data Help

Stock Symbol	Stock Price	Option Symbol	Strike Date	Strike Price	Call Option Premium Bid	Asked	% Gain If Sold	% Gain If Exprd	Mths Till Exp	Best Fit	Break Even Price	Down Side (%)	TAI	Open Intrst
BSC	104.43	BVDLT	12/21/07	100.00	7.20	7.40	2.65	6.89	<1	***	97.23	6.89	TA	8,383
SNDK	38.21	SWQIU	12/21/07	37.50	1.40	1.50	1.81	3.66	<1	*	36.81	3.66	TA	11,233
BSC	104.43	BVDLS	12/21/07	95.00	11.10	11.30	1.60	10.63	<1	*	93.33	10.63	TA	3,298
BSC	104.43	BVDLR	12/21/07	90.00	15.50	15.80	1.02	14.84	<1	*	88.93	14.84	TA	1,416
BSC	104.43	BVDAT	1/18/08	100.00	9.40	9.80	4.76	9.00	1	*	95.03	9.00	TA	8,468
SNKD	38.21	SWQUA	1/18/08	37.50	2.50	2.60	4.78	6.54	1	*	35.71	6.54	TA	8,930
BSC	104.43	BVDAS	1/18/08	95.00	13.00	13.40	3.42	12.45	1	*	91.43	12.45	TA	2,033
BSC	104.43	BVDAR	1/18/08	90.00	17.00	17.40	2.46	16.28	1	*	87.43	16.28	TA	1,578
SNDK	38.21	SWQAG	1/18/08	35.00	4.10	4.30	2.33	10.73	1	*	34.11	10.73	TA	7,354
BSC	104.43	BVDAQ	1/18/08	85.00	21.30	21.80	1.79	20.40	1	*	82.13	20.40	TA	669
BSC	104.43	BVDAP	1/18/08	80.00	25.90	26.30	1.41	24.80	1	*	78.53	24.80	TA	831
BSC	104.43	BVDAO	1/18/08	75.00	20.60	31.00	1.12	29.30	1	*	73.83	29.30	TA	466
SNDK	38.21	SWQDU	4/18/08	37.50	4.80	5.00	10.70	12.56	4	***	33.41	12.56	TA	1,495
BSC	104.43	BVDDT	4/18/08	100.00	14.40	14.70	9.55	13.79	4	***	90.03	13.79	TA	899
SNDK	38.21	SWQDG	4/18/08	35.00	6.20	6.40	7.83	16.23	4	*	32.01	16.23	TA	1,740
BSC	104.43	BVDDS	4/18/08	95.00	17.60	18.00	7.82	16.85	4	*	86.83	16.85	TA	596
BSC	104.43	BVDDR	4/18/08	90.00	21.30	21.60	6.58	20.40	4	*	83.13	20.40	TA	1,216

Call Option Filters

Set Filters then Do for Results.

Set Defaults

Option Premium ($)>= (xx.xx) .10

☑ I-T-M Only   TAI = TA   Best Fit Any

Click Here to add scroll bars if needed

Cancel   Do   UnDo

If Sold Gain(%)>= (xx.xx) 1   <= 30.00 (xx.xx)

If Expired Gain (%) >= (xx.xx) 2.00   <= 30.00 (xx.xx)

Months to Expiration <= (x) 4

Downside Protection % >= (xx.xx) 0

Cancel

THE PUT OPTION SEARCH ENGINE—Displays the put options that meet your strike month, Put Factor, and premium criteria. It also provides the current price, the 52-week trading range, 50-day average, Buy Limit, Buy Rank, TAI, and Beta. A best fit to the Put Factor is calculated along with % discount and months to expiration. The search engine creates a summary of all the options sorted by best Put Factor from all the stocks in your search list.

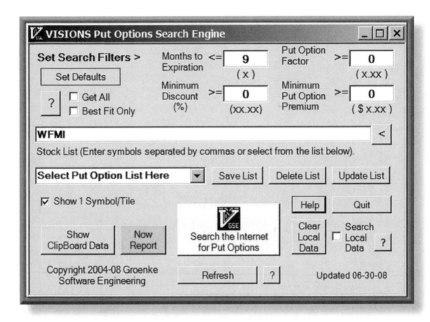

Sample Put Options for one stock WFMI

Put Options for WHOLE FOODS MARKT [WFMI] On 12/10/07 10:08 AM price < 50DayAvg TAI=Bad Idea

Print Throw Away Export Data Get Chart

Put Options for WHOLE FOODS MARKET [WFMI] On 12/10/07 10:08 AM Price < 50DayAvg TAI=Bad Idea
Price 42.87 (-0.18) 52WkHi 53.65 53WkLow 36.00 50DayAvg 42.25 BL 40.41 BR -5.58 Beta 1.15

Option Symbol	Strike Date	Strike Price	Put Option Premium Bid	Asked	Open Interest	Put Factor	Percent Discount	Mths Till Exp	Best Fit	Price If Assigned
FMQXF	12/21/07	30.00	0.02	0.04	1,654	0.43	0.07	<1		29.98
FMQXC	12/21/07	35.00	0.07	0.09	3,287	0.67	0.20	<1		34.93
FMQXH	12/21/07	40.00	0.32	0.35	8,291	0.86	0.80	<1	*	39.68
FMQXI	12/21/07	45.00	2.51	2.57	6,526	-3.86	5.58	<1		42.49
FMQXJ	12/21/07	50.00	7.20	7.35	392	-30.80	14.40	<1		42.80
FMQMF	1/18/08	30.00	0.05	0.07	6,103	0.32	0.17	1		29.95
FMQMG	1/18/08	35.00	0.23	0.25	5,546	0.66	0.66	1		34.77
FMQMH	1/18/08	40.00	0.95	0.99	10,223	0.77	2.38	1	*	39.05
FMQMB	1/18/08	42.50	1.85	1.89	5,754	0.17	4.35	1		40.65
FMQMI	1/18/08	45.00	3.25	3.35	6,289	-1.54	7.22	1		41.75
FMQMC	1/18/08	47.50	5.15	5.30	4,812	-4.76	10.84	1		42.35
FMQMJ	1/18/08	50.00	7.35	7.50	11,016	-9.43	14.70	1		42.65

Put Options filtered and sorted for a list of stocks

Put Options For [INTC,SNDK,GE,BSC,IMCL,]   12-10-07 10:23 AM

Edit Print Data>Clipbd UnDo Show Stk Data Show Bar Graph Sort Put Factor Sort Discnt Sort by Date Filter Throw Away Get/Save Data Help

Stock Symbl	Stock Price	Option Symbol	Strike Date	Strike Price	Put Option Bid	Premium Asked	Put Factor	Dis-Count (%)	Mths Till Exp	Best Fit	Price If Assigned TAI	Open Intrst
BSC	104.12	BVDXS	12/21/07	95.00	1.20	1.30	1.82	1.26	<1	<->	93.80	TA	9,914
BSC	104.12	BVDXR	12/21/07	90.00	0.60	0.70	1.57	0.67	<1	<->	89.40	TA	9,356
BSC	104.12	BVDXT	12/21/07	100.00	2.40	2.45	1.48	2.40	<1	***	97.60	TA	10,492
BSC	104.12	BVDXQ	12/21/07	85.00	0.30	0.40	1.19	0.35	<1	**	84.70	TA	3,498
IMCL	42.30	QCIXH	12/21/07	40.00	0.50	0.60	1.08	1.25	<1	**	39.50	BI	2,436
SNDK	38.16	CEUMF	1/18/08	30.00	1.90	2.25	7.75	6.33	1	<->	28.10	TA	546
SNDK	38.16	CEUMG	1/18/08	35.00	5.60	6.20	6.50	16.00	1	<->	29.40	TA	858
SNDK	38.16	CEUME	1/18/08	25.00	0.20	0.45	1.90	0.80	1	<->	24.80	TA	301
BSC	104.12	BVDMO	1/18/08	75.00	0.75	0.80	1.75	1.00	1	<->	75.25	TA	4,758
BSC	104.12	BVDMQ	1/18/08	85.00	1.45	1.55	1.73	1.71	1	<->	83.55	TA	10,765
BSC	104.12	BCDMP	1/18/08	80.00	1.00	1.10	1.70	1.25	1	<->	79.00	TA	30,144
BSC	104.12	BVDML	1/18/08	60.00	0.30	0.35	1.65	0.50	1	<->	59.70	TA	4,100
BSC	104.12	BVDMR	4/18/08	90.00	2.10	2.20	1.65	2.33	1	<->	87.90	TA	13,924
BSC	104.12	BVDMN	4/18/08	70.00	0.50	0.65	1.57	0.71	1	<->	69.50	TA	2,906
BSC	104.12	BVDMK	4/18/08	55.00	0.20	0.30	1.46	0.36	1	***	54.80	TA	3,671
BSC	104.12	BVDMM	4/18/08	65.00	0.35	0.50	1.46	0.54	1	***	64.65	TA	3,987
BSC	104.12	BVDMS	4/18/08	95.00	3.00	3.30	1.36	3.16	1	***	92.00	TA	6,980

Put Option Filters
Set Filters then Do for Results.

Set Defaults

Copyright 2005 Groenke
Software Engineering

Option Premium ($)>= (xx.xx) .10
TAI Any ▶ Best Fit >Blank ▶

Cancel   Do   UnDo

Click Here to add scroll bars if needed

Put Factor >= (xx.xx) .50
Discout (%) >= (xx.xx) 0.00

Months to Expiration <= (x) 4

Cancel

THE TRADE PLANNER—This tool allows you to prepare a plan for executing a number of Covered Calls and Naked Puts. You can review the overall results (% gain) on your current stock and option selections. You can save and print the plan at any time.

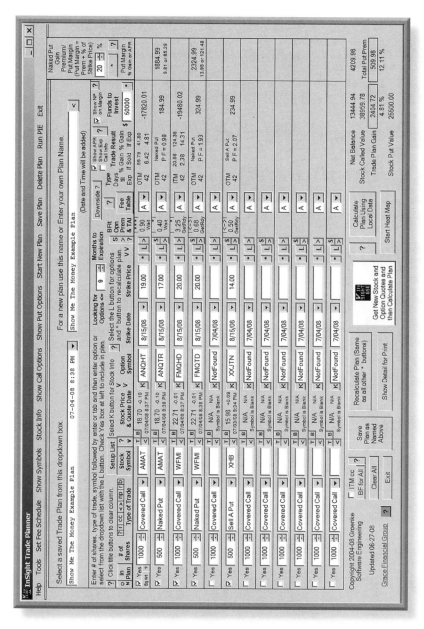

Trade Plan Summary

```
┌─────────────────────────────────────────────────────────────────────┐
│ ⊻ VISIONS Trade Planner Detail Results                      _ □ ✕    │
├─────────────────────────────────────────────────────────────────────┤
│ Print  Find  Calendar  Export Data  Throw Away                        │
├─────────────────────────────────────────────────────────────────────┤

VISIONS INSIGHT TRADE PLAN SUMMARY                          07-04-08

PLAN TITLE: Show Me The Money Example Plan          07-04-08 8:38 PM

DATE      TRANSACTION                              (+/- AMOUNT)     BALANCE
--------  ---------------------------------------  --------------  -----------
07-05-08  INITIAL INVESTMENT                       +    50000.00   50000.00

07-05-08  BUY  1000 APPLIED MATERIALS     @  18.70 -    18705.00   31295.00
          SELL 10  AMAT  AUG 19.00  CALLS @   0.90 +      884.99   32179.99
          CALLED VALUE = 18979.90   SOLD % =  6.42  EXP % =  4.81
          ANQHT, OTM, TAI = Wait            42 Das  to Exp

07-04-08  SELL 5   AMAT  AUG 17.00  PUTS @   0.40 +      184.99   32354.98
          ANQTR, OTM, TAI = Wait, P F = 0.98     42 Days to Exp
          PUT MARGIN @ 20 % = 1884.99    GAIN ON MARGIN = 9.81 %

07-04-08  BUY  1000 WHOLE FOODS MARKT      @  22.71 -    22715.00    9649.98
          SELL 10  WFMI  AUG 20.00  CALLS @   3.25 +     3234.98   12884.96
          CALLED VALUE = 19979.88   SOLD % =  2.38  EXP % = 14.31
          FMQHD, ITM, TAI = GetRdy          42 Days to Exp

07-04-08  SELL 5   WFMI  AUG 20.00  PUTS @   0.68 +      324.99   13209.95
          FMQTD, OTM, TAI = GetRdy, P F = 1.93    42 Days to Exp
          PUT MARGIN @ 20 % = 2324.99    GAIN ON MARGIN = 13.98 %

07-04-08  SELL 5   XHB   AUG 14.00  PUTS @   0.50 +      234.99   13444.94
          XXJTN, OTM, TAI = GetRdy, P F = 2.07    42 Days to Exp

STOCK CALLED ASSIGNMENT VALUES AT STRIKE PRICE ON EXPIRATION DATE

08-15-08  1000    AMAT  CALLED @ 19.00            +    18979.90   18979.90
08-15-08  1000    WFMI  CALLED @ 20.00            +    19979.88   38959.78

STOCK PUT ASSIGNMENT VALUES AT STRIKE PRICE ON EXPIRATION DATE

08-15-08  500     AMAT  PUT ASSIGNED @ 17.00      +     8519.99    8519.99
08-15-08  500     WFMI  PUT ASSIGNED @ 20.00      +    10019.99   18539.98

TOTAL NAKED PUT MARGIN                   4209.98
TOTAL NAKED PUT PREMIUM                   509.98
NAKED PUT GAIN ON MARGIN                 12.11 %

INITIAL INVESTMENT                      50000.00
STOCK CALLED VALUE AT STRIKE PRICE      38959.78
CASH IN ACCOUNT                         13444.94

TOTAL PORTFOLIO GAIN                     2404.72
                                         4.81 %
```

Appendix C

THE VISIONS STOCK EXPLORER—Displays the Stock Data, Call Options, Put Options, and Chart for any one stock. Allows a quick look at all the information for any one company. This is a small view. Run the free trial to see all the features in action.

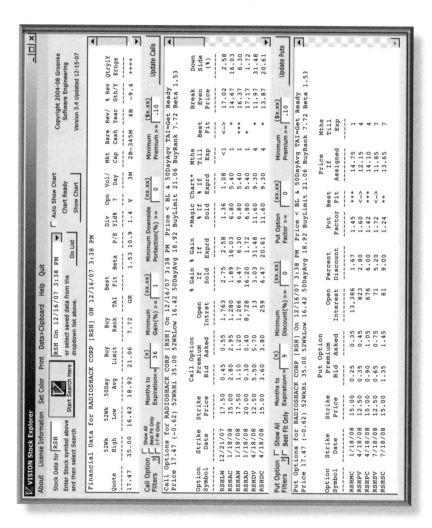

163

THE VISIONS Portfolio Income Explorer (PIE)—Displays the best short-term call options for the list of stocks in any portfolio. Download this and other trial software at **www.RonGroenke.com**.

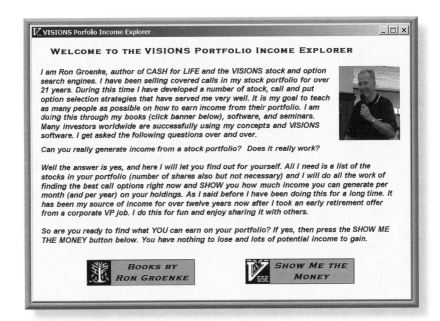

Example of results from the VISIONS Portfolio Income Explorer program

VISIONS Portfolio Income Explorer Results — Prepared 8/27/2008 8:58:04 PM

About Print Save To Clipboard Settings Import a List Retrieve Portfolio Quick List Mgr Adv List Mgr Help Quit

Stock Symbol	# Of Shares	Price Quote	Option Symbol	Strike Date	Strike Price	Call Option Prem	Days Till Exp	Option Income /Month	Called Value	Current Value
SNDA	400	26.63	QKUIF	9/19/08	30.00	0.60	23	313	12000	10652
FMCN	400	31.22	QOHIC	9/19/08	35.00	0.65	23	339	14000	12488
CREE	500	23.39	CQRIE	9/19/08	25.00	0.50	23	326	12500	11695
AEO	700	14.35	AEOIC	9/19/08	15.00	0.35	23	320	10500	10045
RVBD	600	17.14	UEXIW	9/19/08	17.50	0.65	23	509	10500	10284
FOSL	400	29.43	FUAIF	9/19/08	30.00	1.05	23	548	12000	11772
ADSK	300	36.93	ADIU	9/19/08	37.50	0.90	23	352	11250	11079
VPRT	400	32.31	QPYIG	9/19/08	35.00	0.40	23	209	14000	12924
JNPR	400	25.30	JUXIZ	9/19/08	26.00	0.50	23	261	10400	10120
SINA	300	41.81	NOQIN	9/19/08	45.00	0.60	23	235	13500	12543

Retrieve/Manage Portfolio List Here   **Click Here to Learn More**

Select a saved Portfolio Here   Saved Date

Scout Top Ten   8/27/2008 8:57:39 PM

Edit Portfolio   Show Income from Local Data

Delete Portfolio   Create New Portfolio   Show Panel for List Input

Sort By Income | by Symbol

Start Search for New Stock and Option Data

Copyright 2004-08 Groenke Software Engineering

Total Monthly Income	$ 3,411
Total Called Value	$ 120,650
Total Current Value	$ 113,602

See Help on tool bar for more Information

Potential Capital Gain	$ 7,048	
Potential Yearly Income	$ 40,930	36.03%

Scout Top Ten

THE MONEY TREE TOOLS for WRITING COVERED CALLS and NAKED PUTS— Provides Wizards, Worksheets, and other functions that allow you to quickly analyze any prospective call and put option prospect.

CALL OPTION WIZARD—Computes the gain (if called or if expired) from call premiums on various strike prices and expiration dates. Indicates desirable (Magic Chart) premiums.

PUT OPTION WIZARD—Computes the Put Factor for any strike price and strike month combination. This factor is then used to show the premium desired in your selection analysis.

PROSPECT LIST MANAGER—Computes Buy Limit, Buy Rank & Take Action Indicator (TAI) for stocks on your prospect list. Also sort by any column. Gets updates from the Internet when requested.

STOCK and OPTIONS Portfolio SIMULATOR—As described in Chapter 16, generates expected return for any account size, level of margin, call and put premium values and monthly, quarterly or yearly option cycles.

STOCK AND OPTIONS WORKSHEETS—Provides ready to use Excel templates.

OPTION PLAN Worksheet—This worksheet lays out a month-by-month option plan by stock. Call and put premiums are totaled by month and year. Shows the yearly income potential from your holdings.

PROSPECT LIST Worksheet—Provides the stock selection criteria outlined in the book. Calculates the Buy Limit and Buy Rank for your prospects. Use the Excel sort function to sort on any attribute.

STOCK TRANSACTION AND HISTORY FILE Worksheet—Track your trades and summarize your results over time. Sort by stock to track results, like the examples in the book.

THE MONEY TREE STOCK MARKET SIMULATOR—Allows you to forecast your own picture of where the market may be headed. It is based on your own assessment of things, such as interest rates, the employment picture, GDP growth, and other factors. Track your forecast against the actual market performance over time. Use it as a guide for investment decisions.

**More Comments from Investers
and from Seminars**

Investor Comments

My experience with Ron Groenke has been very positive. I picked up Ron's book at Barnes & Noble a few months ago. It was well written and easy to read. Even though I consider myself an experienced investor as I was in the financial planning business for over 10 years, this was the first time I had heard of Ron's concept of using Covered Calls and Naked Puts. The concept immediately made sense to me and I have implemented it with a good deal of success. His Visions software is a great compliment to the strategy. Not only has Ron come up with a great investment strategy, he is a very nice, honest man who is obviously passionate about his system.

Mike Conlon
Cary, NC 27511

Ron's book is an excellent tool for any one with an interest in finance and individual money management. I recommend the book to many of my friends who ask me for advice on investing. It is an easy read and lays the foundation for a safe and wise approach to a piece of any investment strategy. I encourage students in the introductory investments class to read the book as it can be read in just a few days. The software is user friendly and has provided a consistent return for me in each of the years I have used it and followed the conservative investing strategies outlined in the book.

Dr. Richard Rawlins PhD
Professor Finance & Economics
Missouri Southern State University
Joplin, MO 64801

No hard sell or bluster, just honest results. I have studied Ron's books and have attended his latest seminar. Employing Ron Groenke's system of option strategies has increased my return significantly without increasing my risk. Ron makes sense and is for real.

John Scott
Marco Island, FL

As a Realtor for 40 years, (since retired) I've invested in every conceivable investment vehicle over the years. Ron's *Show Me the Money* is the only book that shows you how to get paid up front, rather than having to wait for the market to go up or down. Ron's formulas are straight forward, and the software does all the work. I love it!

Gordon Bolton
Pleasant Hill, CA 94523

I have bought 3 of Ron's books including *Show Me the Money: Covered Calls & Naked Puts for a Monthly Cash Income.* I find them very informative and explain very easily how to trade Covered Calls for a very nice monthly income. I have attended several seminars, which provides me with additional insight to trading Ron's methods. The software has been very helpful in finding potential trades. Since I have been using Ron's methods I have put cash into my accounts each and every month, which I am compounding the income to do more trades. I am really glad I ran across Ron's trading methods. Ron, keep the good work up!

Richard Power
New Port Richey, FL

In the past two years since I discovered Ron Groenke's book, *Show Me the Money: Covered Calls & Naked Puts for a Monthly Cash Income* and his accompanying software [VISIONS], I have increased my investment income almost three-fold and virtually without risk. The investment marketplace is littered with thousands of books, newsletters, and software systems and I have bought and tried many of them. What Ron has done is cut through the clutter with a common sense approach to maximizing income through investment. I highly recommend this book.

Bruce Davis
Addison, TX 75001

I am very happy with the software and the book. I've been using the software for some time now with a high win ratio. These tools are a *must* have for any investor with little time and a conservative attitude.

Blake Hansen, CEO,
DBN Securities P/L, Australia

Investor Comments

As a Finance Professor, I wish that I had written this book.

The beauty of Ron's work is its straightforwardness and ease of replication. Ron presents a methodology of capital market trading in a readable, understandable, and achievable manner. I have both presented his technique in the classroom and have adopted it personally. Simply stated, Ron's methods really work.

Harry F. Griffin PhD
Troy University Montgomery
Montgomery, AL 36103.

Don't buy *Show Me the Money* UNLESS you want to make money trading stocks and options! Groenke's basic philosophy of making small gains consistently is the name of the game. Slow and steady wins the race! And VISIONS software makes it easy to find the right stocks and options. Do yourself a favor: Buy *Show Me the Money*, follow its principles, watch your account balance grow dramatically in only a few months. I use the book as the primary text in a Financial Freedom class I teach; it's terrific and my students love it!

Richard Gooudeau
Macon, GA

Ron's insights and thorough process of evaluating investments for income through options has been refreshing and profitable for me. I've employed his method for over a year and am happily supplementing my investment income through Covered Calls. For experienced investors, Ron's method is a terrific addition to anyone's wealth creation toolkit. I recommend Ron and his program wholeheartedly to investors looking for successful and wise investment strategies.

Nalini C. Indorf Kaplan
Boulder, CO

I just wanted to get my feet wet doing Covered Calls. I bought *Cash for Life* along with Visions Software. Visions Walk was very helpful in showing how to use the software. I'm well on my way to 15% a *month* return on my initial investments.

Jim Robertello
Forest Hill, MD 21050

I think Ron's book, *Show Me the Money*, is the best Covered Calls book I have read. I have read many investment related books and I have attended several stock and options trading workshops and when I read Ron's book, a light bulb really went off as far as writing options vs. buying options as a speculator. I also like his software [VISIONS] for its simplicity and ease of use. I hope to attend your workshop later this year when time permits. I have recommended Ron's book to many friends too.

David B. Lunn
Westlake Village, CA

I am extremely new to the world of options trading and your book and the seminar opened my eyes to a rather straightforward con-servative approach to options trading, how to do it and what my expectations might be for the future (although there are no guaran-tees). I thoroughly enjoyed the seminar and I have never witnessed such an involved or attentive group of people eager to absorb the information you presented. I think that there is a lot more that I will learn because I intend to repeat the class exercise in detail. I am looking forward to seminars that you might present in the future, but next time I'll be bringing some of my relatives in tow so that they can learn the value of trading Covered Calls and Naked Puts.

Richard Short
Dunedin, FL

I bought one of Ron's books [*The Money Tree: Risk Free Options Trading*] about 5–6 years ago. I found the strategies compelling. I then bought Ron's *Cash for Life* when I took over management of managing my wife's IRA in August 2007. A very volatile time, late 2007, I researched from a cash position, where to invest and apply the strategies.

I made a 7 percent return in 3 months with a six figure position doing Covered Calls in March 2008.

Patrick J Swint, MS, PA-C
Major, US Air Force, retired
Austin, Texas

Investor Comments

I used another company's investing software, and took their classes. However, I felt lost in how to really invest. I read Ron Groenke's *Show Me the Money* book, and it was like a light went on. I actually had formulas to use and concepts I could understand. The seminar was great in it helped explain all of the software's functionality. I wouldn't use any other software.

Denise Stein
Smyrna, GA 30082

After reading Ron Groenke's book *Show Me the Money: Covered Calls & Naked Puts for a Monthly Cash Income*, I started looking at investments in an entirely different light. I like the way Ron's approach is very systematic and process-oriented. I also purchased his software and using it alongside the principles I learned in the book, I no longer second-guessed any of my investment decisions. I knew that the process would determine the proper investment and covered call at the given time.

Bert Maqueda
Waco, TX 76712

In these times of increased uncertainty and greater volatility it is reassuring to know that, thanks to Ron through his books, seminars and software, we have the ability to make money regardless of what the stock market is doing. In his latest book *Show Me the Money: Covered Calls & Naked Puts for a Monthly Cash Income* he has distilled a complex subject into easy to understand tools and methodology for generating a regular income from stocks whether you own them or not."

Roger Hay
Morgan Hill, CA 95037

My Name is Jackie Miller and I'm 79 years of age. I live in San Antonio, TX 78260. My A G Edwards stockbroker gave me Ron's first book to read. I have been in the market off and on for 45 years. I just have done fair, but I never found a method I really liked till I got Ron's Book *Show Me the Money*. It changed my way of investing.

Jackie Miller
San Antonio, TX

I read *Cash for Life* a year ago and it really opened my eyes to a sector of the market that seemed obtuse and dangerous. Ron's explanations and the Visions software have provided me a lot of help in managing a rather complex set of investments. Even though I am working with a full service broker, this book has furthered my ability to communicate effectively with the broker. Thanks very much.

Pope Lawrence
Merced, CA

Ron Groenke's book and software take what is often considered a complicated and risky investment strategy and provides a framework to learn and implement a proven methodology. Using a simple storyline, he takes a difficult subject and makes it accessible. As long as you do your due diligence, these tools make the process of finding good opportunities for covered call writing and cash secured puts relatively easy, and will result in a monthly cash flow, depending on your personal risk tolerance and resources.

S.G.
Ontario, Canada

In April, 2006 I attended Ron's seminar. That experience along with his book, *Show Me the Money: Covered Calls & Naked Puts for a Monthly Cash Income* has increased my portfolio 54%. The software is user friendly and regularly updated. Ron responds by email to my questions within a day.

Richard Hamad
Sagamore Hills, OH

I have been trading stocks, options and futures for a number of years. One problem I have had is finding something safe for my retirement funds yet make those funds grow. Covered call writing is one of the safest ways there is but finding the right combination of stocks and options is time consuming and difficult. When I read Ron's book *Cash for Life* I thought his approach with its precise rules was just what I was looking for. I purchased Ron's Vision software which applies the *Cash for Life* rules. The results were amazing. If you are looking for a systematic approach to investing that is predictable and safe, this is the program.

Geof Kressin
Knoxville, TN 37902

I have been so impressed with the VISIONS software and with Ronald Groenke's trading knowledge that I attended one of his seminar's in November 2007. Since that time, I have utilized his system for all of my trading decisions. I have been actively trading for the last 12 years and have read innumerable books regarding the market. Of the dozens of books I have studied, I personally feel that Ronald Groenke's system and VISIONS software are the most effective method of trading to be able to maximize profits and limit any losses. I would like to thank you for all of the help your book has given me in continuing my development as a successful trader!

Bob Anderson
|Murray, Utah

I have been with Ron for about three years now, so I know that using the system detailed in *Show Me the Money* gives me the house odds in the mad casino we call the stock market. Best of all though is Ron's unstinting personal support for his customers.

Tim Paskvan
Stillwater, MN 55082

Show Me the Money is a very readable introduction to these low-risk strategies for producing an income stream from one's portfolio. The methodology is sound, well explained in the book and well implemented in the software. The book, the software, and Ron's seminar are great values.

Chris Walker
Clearwater, FL

I read both of Ron Groenke's earlier books, *Cash for Life* and *Covered Calls and Naked Puts*, enjoyed them thoroughly, and learned a great deal about Covered Calls and Naked Puts. I purchased Ron's VISIONS software and proceeded to utilize the software with moderate success, profiting on seventy percent of my trades. The real success came when I attended Ron's seminar in Naples FL last year and learned the true power of the VISIONS software. I sincerely urge anybody that wants to utilize the full power of the VISIONS software to attend Ron's class. Its money well spent.

Skip Toombs
Canandaigua, NY

177

I've been trading Covered Calls for over two decades. Since reading Ron's book and using his system, I've been placing more trades and getting a better return. As an engineer, I always search for the easiest, most effective method in whatever I undertake and Ron's system is elegant in its simplicity. I highly recommend *Show Me the Money* and VISIONS software.

Robert Bickford
Dallas, TX

Seminar Comments

Ron's seminar provided me with a "hands-on" approach to options, without all the complexity one normally is exposed to when dealing with this subject. More so it revealed how to use options in a conservative way, the opposite of what I had always associated with options.

Hans Grether
Sao Paulo, Brazil

It is rare to have the knowledge *and* the ability to pass it on to others who don't have the background and experience in such a way that they can comprehend and use the information. Ron has got it!

L J Strope
Wheaton, IL

Before coming to the seminar I did not know the power of VISIONS. It is a very powerful tool. I enjoyed the class. I learned about the recovery process that was really helpful.

Jackie Mason
Duluth, GA

This is the second seminar that I have attended and I can't begin to tell you how much I refined my knowledge of trading and working with the software. This is a wonderful, conservative approach to the wide world of investments.

David Lambson
Cherry Hill, NJ

Each time I am with Ron, it is a new learning experience and he makes a complex subject extremely simple.

Arnold L. Weiner
Lincolnwood, IL

Wonderful seminar, good materials and great presentation. Lots of actual trades by Ron are easy to follow and form a good path to learning. I really enjoyed the actual placing of real orders in real time. Actually did the UNG Naked Put right along with Ron for 10 contracts. Will pay for seminar I hope. The trade planner is extremely versatile and has numerous whistles and bells, almost too many to learn at one time. I will need more time and hands on practice to really get all of its power.

Walter Toombs
Canandaigua, NY

Ron has turned his passion for investing with Covered Calls into a book and seminar that he is willing to share with others to help them enhance their financial well-being.

Louis Ciullo
Brielle, NJ

As with most experts in any field, Ron's book and seminar represent many years of experience in Covered Calls and Naked Puts. What is unique and refreshing is that Ron not only thoroughly knows his subject, he is completely candid and honest. You can rely on and believe in what he says.

John Scott
Marco Island, FL

The seminar was a fast-paced, very thorough walk through of VISIONS software, a series of search engines to help investors to better understand Ron Groenke's concepts about selling options.

David Dolgin
Tampa, FL

Ron is a man of patience, persistence and principle which comes through to readers and students in his books and seminars. His program is amazingly effective! Many thanks to Ron for making his knowledge available to new investors. I used Ron's Visions software for a year before I attended his seminar. I had amazing results by following Ron's careful and thoughtful plan. The Visions software is an invaluable tool that helps me define, analyze, and select the right stocks for my portfolio.

Marie Kennedy
Phoenix, AZ

Thank you Ron for leading the seminar. The VISIONS software is very impressive and powerful. You made options (covered Calls and Naked Puts) easy to understand. It's obvious that you really want to help your students understand your principles. You & Jean are terrific.

**John George
Hudson, WI**

Great seminar. It really helped me get more familiar with the VISIONS tools. VISIONS has been a great benefit to me to learn how to trade Covered Calls. Great information and a good price. Thanks Ron.

**Bob Morley
Moroni, UT**

I found your books on Amazon, read them and used the trial period on VISIONS and knew immediately this was a common sense way to evaluate covered call opportunities and stocks as well. The seminar was all I had hoped for. Thank you for a very well organized instruction without any "sales Hype" or "showmanship."
PS: You passed the acid test. I have made enough money using your program to pay for the seminar, books and software subscription before coming to the seminar. Thanks!!

**L J Strope
Wheaton, IL**

I enjoyed the seminar. It was nice to get an in-depth overview of the VISIONS software. I had used parts of VISIONS but wasn't familiar with all the features. I also liked the actual trading done in the class. It was good to go from the beginning of looking for stocks through the analysis of the data, and actually making decisions. It was nice that you share everything you do like the spreadsheets and recording of transactions. I can't think of anything that I would have liked to see done differently. I think everything was covered.

**Denise Stein
Smyrna, GA**

Ron's genius ability with stocks, computers and Covered Calls was very evident. He shared his knowledge. I like his plan of picking fruit ($$) from different money trees.

**Phillip Bressinck
Southlake, TX**

Ron is great at answering individual questions. He is very patient (at least externally) in dealing with the students. By far the most valuable part of the seminar was when Ron took the class through an actual search, evaluation and trade. Getting inside a trader's head is the greatest learning tool and following his thinking through a trade really helped with the "art" aspect of selling Covered Calls. His after hours accessibility is also a unique and valuable feature. Thank you for another great learning experience.

Fred Schadler Ph.D.
Greenville, NC

One reason I attended this seminar was because I thought I was not aware of the power of some of the analytical software of VISIONS. I'm glad I attended the seminar because I learned a great deal about investing philosophy and ways to use Ron's search engines and "what if" planners.

W.A. Burns
Canfield, OH

The seminar was very informative and presented calls and puts in a simple and easy to follow format. *Show Me The Money* is an essential book for any investor. Ron seems to plan for and share improvements as they evolve. Y'all were great hosts!

Wil Wilhite
Arkansas

A lot of meat. "The beef was here." The entire seminar deals with specific info rather than generalities. This provides far a very good learning experience. This is my third Ron Groenke seminar and they just keep getting better. I will look forward to the next one.

Dale Anderson
Muncy, PA

I appreciate the time, energy and knowledge that went into developing this program. It made analysis much easier. The best part is that Ron is unassuming and it is comforting to know that he shares real data and experiences from his trading. A great workshop!

Nello Vignocchi
Flossmoor, IL

Seminar very well organized! Materials very consistent with sessions. Easy to follow and questions were answered well. The best part for me was that I did not feel intimidated and I expected to be. The attitude and atmosphere was one of facilitating the learner. Ron ... great guy. Ego very under control. So much accomplished, yet humble and helpful. Very comfortable with the material because it is yours. Not teaching a theory—very practical and hands on. Thanks so much. I would definitely attend again.

Carol Koogler
Gainesville, FL

Great presentation. Lots of material. It will take several days to digest what I've learned and review VISIONS many features.

Paul Messerschmidt
Tampa, FL

After reading the book and attending the seminar I feel enabled to begin trading Covered Calls and Naked Puts. I now have a plan and method to begin.

Doug Errington
Naples, FL

Meet the Author
Ronald Groenke

RON GROENKE moved from Minnesota to the sunny gulf coast community of Marco Island after twenty-five years in the communications systems and software development environment. He has been active in the stock options market for over twenty five years and developed the concepts and techniques provided in this book.

On Marco, he and wife, Jean, are active in their church and busy entertaining family and friends who visit from the north.

Besides options investing/advising, other activities include personal computing, walking, boating, and volunteer work.

Ron can be reached at **Ron@RonGroenke.com**